Every human: Advocate for World Peace

DM Ole Kiminta

Published by KBros, 2025.

EVERY HUMAN: ADVOCATE FOR WORLD PEACE

First edition. March 26, 2025.

Copyright © 2025 DM Ole Kiminta.

ISBN: 978-1069323156

Written by DM Ole Kiminta.

Also by DM Ole Kiminta

How the Western Democracies failed the world
Supporting Refugees in their Homelands
Dissuading Global War Mongers:
Dissuading war mongers
La Libération Monétaire en Afrique
Canada Post: Management failure to modernise mail systems
Canada Post management failure to modernise mail systems
Canada Post: Management failure to modernise mail systems
Live to be 200
Aim to live for 200
Aim to live to be 200
Western democracies failed the world economies
Wrong foot forward: US-Canada trade wars
Canada begs to differ: Never a 51st state of USA
Tethered to the Kitchen
Nous ne pouvons pas être le 51e État des États-Unis
Nous ne serons jamais le 51ème état des États-Unis.
The Nephilim and the erosion of moral boundaries
Every human is an advocate for World Peace
The diplomatic dilemma of Western Sahara
Every human: Advocate for World Peace

Table of Contents

Every human is an advocate for world peace

(Second Edition)

DM Ole Kiminta

Chapter 1: Necessity of a credible World Order

At our present troubling time in our attempts to tame the world's war mongering nations, if we abandon the sincere certainty of establishing a genuine world peace at any rate, it is likely to leave us with a skeptical paradox that will obviously be depressing and deplorable to say the least. We must never shy away from this bold idea of human freedom. Some governments choose to ignore international law and could care less about antagonising other world nations who keep striving for peace and diplomatic solutions and negotiations in good faith and paradoxically, there seems to be only silence from the so-called international community while defenceless groups of people get squashed and bombed and their homes shredded and levelled to the ground. How can this be? What did we learn from the agonies and sorrows of the last two world wars? We definitely need a world order led by credible and sincere nations that would put the interest of world peace first.

For those who will read what I have written in these few chapters about our fears and loathness to violence and unpalatable squabbles of never-ending conflicts on our planet, I am only expressing my simple and humble opinion on what I have witnessed for a long time since I first exited the world of deplorable colonial illegal occupations, subjugation, exploitation and domination. My views of this issue about world peace might be different from yours, I respect that so profoundly.

One of the greatest predicaments for current generation is the inherent uncertainty and difficulty in understanding and navigating complex situations for world peace where solutions might seem quite elusive while the potential consequences are significant. The puzzle for the new generation worldwide is the absence of world peace, a priceless entity that can never return equal to the demand if not availed to them by us, that is, if we can halt the speeding train of those who are carrying big guns gluttonously. The 'Cell-phone generation' has never experienced real world peace that existed before the world wars. How do we define it to them? In my view, every living human on this planet is an advocate for the world peace, a priceless commodity.

Understanding credibility in global governance is essential for fostering a cooperative international environment where nations can thrive. Credibility refers not only to the reliability of states in fulfilling their commitments but also to the trustworthiness of international institutions and agreements. As countries navigate the complexities of globalisation, the need for a credible world order becomes increasingly apparent. A world where nations can depend on one another to uphold their obligations is crucial for peace, economic stability, and the collective well-being of humanity.

Overview of the book's structure

This book is the second edition of 'Every human is an advocate for world peace'. Some important elements of the subject had been left out (chapter 5 and chapter 6) and had not been availed for publication and had to be corrected prodigiously for clarity and is now included in this second edition. This book is structured to provide a comprehensive analysis of the complexities surrounding superpowers and their role in global peacekeeping. Each chapter is designed to delve into specific themes that outline the limitations and failures of superpowers in maintaining international peace, illustrating that their actions often hinder rather than help global stability. The organisation of the book allows readers to systematically grasp the multifaceted issues that arise when superpowers engage in peacekeeping efforts, setting the stage for a critical examination of their credibility.

The first section addresses the fundamental question of why current superpowers cannot qualify as credible world peacekeepers. It examines the underlying motivations that drive superpowers to intervene in international conflicts, often prioritising their interests over genuine peacekeeping efforts. This chapter lays the groundwork for understanding the paradox of superpower involvement in peacekeeping missions, highlighting the gap between their stated objectives and the consequences of their actions.

Following this introduction, the book turns to historical failures of superpowers in peacekeeping missions. By analysing key case studies, this section reveals patterns of miscalculations and unintended outcomes that have characterised superpower interventions. These historical examples serve not only to illustrate past mistakes but also to inform current debates about the efficacy and legitimacy of superpower-led peacekeeping initiatives. Readers will gain insights into how these failures have shaped contemporary views on international intervention. On the other hand, there will be those opposed to my opinion and my view of the political calamity in which we are submerged and the unpalatable economic turmoil that we currently find ourselves in, every reader has an opinion which I profoundly accept and try re-examining my opinion and suggestions and topics that I have narrated on this topic.

The impact of military intervention on global stability is the focus of the next chapter. Here, the book discusses the often-destabilising effects that arise from superpower military actions. It argues that military interventions, rather than fostering peace, frequently exacerbate existing tensions and contribute to prolonged conflict. This analysis is critical for understanding the broader implications of superpower behaviour in international relations, particularly in regions already fraught with instability.

Chapters explore the influence of economic sanctions and the dynamics of superpower rivalries on multilateral peacekeeping efforts. Economic sanctions are scrutinised for their effectiveness as tools for conflict resolution, demonstrating that they can lead to unintended humanitarian crises and further entrench hostilities. Additionally, the book examines how superpower rivalries complicate multilateral peacekeeping frameworks, often leading to paralysis in international institutions designed to foster cooperation.

The final chapters bring about a topic which itself is a contributor and an attribute to global problems that result into war and displacements of many innocent people. This topic is on illegal occupation of a country by another country using military force. The last chapter of the book is a lengthy topic with a touchy subject about hawkish aggressive nations as shown on the following lines: 'Hawk's shadow':

The Hawk's Shadow delves into the complex dynamics of international relations, focusing on how aggressive nations contribute to the fragmentation of world peace. This chapter examines the military strategies employed by these hawkish nations, revealing the underlying motivations and tactics that drive their actions. By analysing various regional conflicts that arise from hawkish diplomacy, the chapter highlights the broader implications of these aggressive behaviours on global stability. Through historical case studies, the chapter illustrates the patterns and consequences of militaristic approaches, providing readers with a comprehensive understanding of the challenges facing world peace today.

At the core of the chapter is an exploration of the military strategies utilised by aggressive nations. These strategies often prioritise power projection and dominance over diplomatic engagement, leading to a cycle of conflict and retaliation. The chapter outlines how these nations leverage their military capabilities to assert influence, intimidate adversaries, and secure resources, frequently at the expense of peaceful coexistence. By dissecting these strategies, readers gain insight into the mindset of hawkish leaders and the rationale behind their decision-making processes.

This part of the text also addresses the regional conflicts that stem from hawkish diplomacy, illustrating how aggressive postures can escalate tensions and lead to prolonged violence. The topic presents specific case studies where aggressive nations have intervened in regional disputes, often exacerbating existing tensions.

The analysis reveals a pattern of disregard for international norms and the consequences that ensue, such as humanitarian crises and destabilised regions. This examination underscores the interconnectedness of global security and the ripple effects that aggressive actions can have far beyond national borders.

Historical case studies serve as pivotal examples throughout the book, providing context and depth to the discussion of aggressive nations and their impact on world peace. By examining past conflicts, the narrative illustrates how similar patterns of aggression have repeatedly undermined efforts for diplomacy and reconciliation. These case studies not only highlight the lessons learned from history but also serve as warnings for the present and future. This chapter emphasises the importance of understanding historical precedents to better navigate current geopolitical challenges.

Ultimately, the topic calls for a critical reassessment of how aggressive nations approach international relations. By shedding light on the fragmentation of world peace caused by militaristic strategies, it also advocates for a shift towards diplomacy and cooperation. It urges policymakers, scholars, and the public to recognise the importance of fostering dialogue and understanding to prevent future conflicts. In doing so, it aims to contribute to a more peaceful global landscape, encouraging a collective effort to address the root causes of aggression and promote sustainable solutions for world peace.

By the conclusion of the book, readers will have a nuanced understanding of the consequences of unilateral actions in international conflicts and the urgent need for re-evaluating the role of superpowers in global peacekeeping.

International law plays a pivotal role in establishing this credibility by providing a framework for cooperation and conflict resolution. Treaties, conventions, and agreements serve as the backbone of international relations, setting clear expectations and norms for behaviour among nations. When states adhere to international law, they reinforce their credibility, fostering an environment where dialogue and collaboration can flourish. The consistent application of these laws not only enhances trust between nations but also empowers them to address global challenges collaboratively, from climate change to security threats.

Globalisation has transformed the landscape of national sovereignty and world order, urging states to reconsider their roles within a more interconnected framework. While some may perceive globalisation as a threat to sovereignty, it also offers opportunities for nations to collaborate in addressing shared challenges. The credibility of a world order hinges on the capacity of states to balance their national interests with their responsibilities to the global community. By embracing a credible world order, nations can effectively navigate the complexities of globalisation, ensuring that their sovereignty is complemented by a commitment to collective progress.

Emerging technologies are reshaping international relations and governance, presenting both opportunities and challenges for credibility in global governance. Innovations in communication, data sharing, and artificial intelligence can facilitate transparency and collaboration among nations. However, they also raise questions about security, privacy, and the potential for misuse. To maintain credibility in this rapidly evolving landscape, states must commit to ethical standards and frameworks that govern the use of technology in international relations. By doing so, they can build trust and cooperation while addressing the risks associated with technological advancements.

Cultural diplomacy and military alliances further underscore the significance of credibility in fostering a stable world order. Cultural exchanges can bridge gaps between nations, enhancing mutual understanding and respect, while military alliances provide a foundation for collective security. Both elements contribute to a credible world order by promoting stability and cooperation. As countries navigate the complexities of a fractured world, recognising the importance of cultural ties and strategic partnerships will be paramount. By prioritising credibility in these spheres, nations can work together to create a more peaceful and prosperous global community.

The consequences of a fragmented world

The consequences of a fragmented world are profound and far-reaching, impacting not only national interests but also the global community at large. In a world marked by division and disunity, nations often find themselves embroiled in conflicts that undermine the foundations of international cooperation. This fragmentation leads to a significant erosion of trust among nations, making it increasingly difficult to address pressing global issues such as climate change, public health crises, and economic instability. The urgency of building a credible world order has never been greater, as the consequences of inaction will reverberate across generations.

Globalisation, while offering opportunities for economic growth and cultural exchange, has also contributed to the fragmentation of the world order. As nations grapple with the complexities of maintaining their sovereignty amid interconnectedness, they often prioritise national interests over collaborative efforts. This tendency can lead to a decline in multilateral agreements, weakening the frameworks that support international law. Without a commitment to shared norms and regulations, the potential for conflict escalates, and the ability to tackle global challenges diminishes significantly.

The rapid development of cybersecurity threats, artificial intelligence, and digital warfare has introduced new dimensions to national security concerns, often exacerbating existing tensions between states. In a fragmented world, the lack of cohesive regulations regarding these technologies can lead to mistrust and miscalculations among nations. It is essential for countries to engage in dialogue and establish credible frameworks that govern technological innovation, ensuring that these advancements serve the collective good rather than deepen divisions.

Economic stability is intricately linked to the credibility of world order. A fragmented global economy, marked by trade wars and protectionist policies, creates an environment of uncertainty that impacts growth and development. Countries that engage in cooperative economic practices often experience greater stability and prosperity. By fostering trust and collaboration, nations can build resilient economic systems that not only benefit their citizens but also contribute to a more cohesive international community. The pursuit of a credible world order requires a collective commitment to economic interdependence that transcends national boundaries.

Cultural diplomacy plays a vital role in bridging divides and fostering understanding between nations. In a world that often emphasizes differences, the promotion of shared values and mutual respect can pave the way for greater cooperation. By leveraging cultural exchanges and dialogue, nations can build relationships that transcend political disagreements. This emphasis on cultural understanding, paired with strong military alliances, can establish a foundation for peace and stability. In navigating the challenges of a fractured world, it is crucial for nations to recognise the importance of unity in diversity and work towards a credible world order that reflects the shared aspirations of humanity.

Chapter 2: The role of international law

Foundations of international law

International law serves as the bedrock upon which a credible world order is built. It establishes the rules and principles governing the interactions between states, creating a framework that can foster cooperation and resolve disputes. This legal foundation is critical in an increasingly interconnected world, where the actions of one nation can have far-reaching implications for others. By adhering to international law, nations can cultivate trust and predictability in their relations, essential elements in promoting peace and stability. As states work together to address global challenges, the commitment to a shared legal framework empowers them to navigate complexities and find common ground.

The rise of globalisation has transformed the traditional notions of sovereignty and governance. As countries become more interdependent, the influence of international law grows, necessitating a balance between national interests and global responsibilities. Nations must recognise that their actions are interconnected; what happens in one part of the world can ripple across borders. This realisation encourages states to engage in cooperative strategies and embrace international legal norms that prioritise collective well-being over isolationist tendencies. By reinforcing their commitment to international law, nations can enhance their credibility and strengthen the global order.

Emerging technologies present both opportunities and challenges for international relations and governance. As advancements reshape communication, commerce, and security, the need for a robust legal framework becomes even more pressing. Cybersecurity, artificial intelligence, and biotechnology raise questions that transcend national borders, demanding cooperation and adherence to international norms. States must work collaboratively to develop regulations that address these technological challenges while promoting innovation and protecting human rights. By doing so, they can ensure that technological progress contributes positively to global stability and trust in the international system.

Economic stability is intricately linked to the credibility of the world order. Nations that prioritise adherence to international law are more likely to foster environments conducive to trade, investment, and economic growth. As countries engage in economic partnerships, the rule of law helps to mitigate risks and build confidence among investors and stakeholders. In this context, a credible world order not only promotes peace but also enhances economic opportunities for all nations involved. By recognising the symbiotic relationship between legal frameworks and economic stability, countries can create a more prosperous global community.

Mechanisms for enforcement and compliance

In the quest to establish a credible world order, effective mechanisms for enforcement and compliance are essential. Nations must recognise that adherence to international laws and agreements is not merely a matter of obligation but a pathway to building trust and fostering cooperation. When countries commit to shared norms and frameworks, they lay the foundation for a stable and predictable international environment. This collective adherence enhances global stability, reduces the likelihood of conflict, and promotes a culture of mutual respect. By putting enforcement mechanisms in place, nations can hold each other accountable, reinforcing the credibility of international agreements and fostering a sense of security amongst their citizens.

International law plays a pivotal role in establishing mechanisms for enforcement and compliance. Treaties and conventions provide legal frameworks that nations can rely upon to resolve disputes and uphold commitments. Institutions such as the International Court of Justice and the International Criminal Court serve as platforms for adjudicating conflicts and ensuring that states adhere to their international obligations. By empowering these institutions, countries can create a more robust enforcement architecture that deters violations and encourages compliance. Moreover, the involvement of international organisations fosters collaboration among nations, enabling them to address shared challenges and work towards common goals, thus reinforcing the credibility of the world order.

The impact of globalisation cannot be overstated when discussing enforcement and compliance mechanisms. As nations become increasingly interconnected, their actions have far-reaching consequences that transcend borders. This interconnectedness necessitates a collaborative approach to governance, where compliance with international norms is essential for addressing global issues such as climate change, human rights, and trade. Emerging technologies further complicate this landscape, as they create both opportunities and challenges for international relations. Countries must adapt their enforcement strategies to account for the rapid pace of technological advancement, ensuring that regulations remain relevant and effective in an evolving world.

Economic stability is closely tied to the credibility of world order, and strong enforcement mechanisms are vital in maintaining that stability. When nations comply with international economic agreements and adhere to trade regulations, they foster an environment conducive to investment and growth. Conversely, violations of these agreements can lead to economic turmoil and undermine global confidence in the system. By prioritizing compliance and implementing effective enforcement measures, countries can not only protect their own economic interests but also contribute to a more stable and prosperous global economy.

By fostering mutual understanding and collaboration among diverse cultures, nations can build the trust necessary for effective governance. Simultaneously, military alliances, such as NATO, provide a framework for collective security that enhances global peace and order. These alliances can act as deterrents against aggression and promote adherence to international norms. Ultimately, a credible world order relies on the collective efforts of nations, bolstered by robust mechanisms for enforcement and compliance, to navigate the complexities of a fractured world and work towards a brighter, more cooperative future.

Chapter 3: Globalisation and national sovereignty

The relationship between globalisation and sovereignty presents a complex yet enriching dynamic that shapes the contemporary world order. As nations become increasingly interconnected through trade, technology, and cultural exchange, the traditional notions of sovereignty are being challenged and redefined. This interplay emphasises the need for a credible world order that can effectively address both the benefits and drawbacks of globalisation. Embracing this duality allows nations to harness the advantages of globalisation while safeguarding their sovereignty, ultimately fostering trust among states. In my view, when each nation identifies itself as unique in its own way yet embraces the global identity amiably, it ultimately fosters a closeness and trust in a defined way.

Globalisation has undeniably enhanced economic interdependence, which can serve as a foundation for greater cooperation among nations. As countries engage in international trade and investment, they find common ground that transcends borders, leading to shared prosperity. However, this interdependence also raises concerns about the erosion of national sovereignty. To counter these challenges, nations must work collaboratively to establish international laws and frameworks that respect individual state sovereignty while promoting collective interests. By doing so, they can create a credible world order that balances globalisation with the need for autonomy.

Economic interdependence can lead to greater peace and collaboration, as nations recognize that their prosperity is intertwined. However, economic crises can also lead to isolationist policies and a breakdown of trust among nations. To build a credible world order, it is imperative that countries work together to address economic disparities and create equitable systems that promote growth and stability for all. This requires not only cooperation but also a commitment to fair trade practices and shared economic goals.

Chapter 4: Emerging technologies and their impact

Globalisation, propelled by digital advancements, has further complicated the notion of national sovereignty. As information and goods flow seamlessly across borders, states find themselves in a web of interdependence that can both empower and constrain their actions. This interconnectedness necessitates a revaluation of traditional notions of sovereignty, prompting nations to collaborate more closely on issues that transcend borders, such as climate change, cybersecurity, and public health. By embracing a credible world order, nations can better navigate these complexities, ensuring that their sovereignty is respected while also recognizing their obligations to the global community.

Moreover, the role of non-state actors, including multinational corporations and civil society organizations, has grown significantly in shaping the governance landscape. These entities often wield substantial influence, sometimes surpassing that of traditional state actors. Their involvement in technology development and deployment can lead to innovative solutions but also raises questions about accountability and power dynamics. Encouraging dialogue among all stakeholders, including non-state actors, can lead to more inclusive governance structures that reflect diverse perspectives and foster greater trust among nations.

In conclusion, while the governance challenges posed by new technologies are significant, they also present an opportunity for nations to come together and forge a credible world order. By embracing collaboration, strengthening international law, and engaging non-state actors, countries can address the complexities of the modern technological landscape. This collective effort will not only enhance global stability but also promote a more equitable distribution of technological benefits, ultimately reinforcing trust and cooperation among nations.

Chapter 5: Military alliances and global peace

Alliances play a crucial role in maintaining order in the international system, serving as a cornerstone for collective security and cooperation among nations. By forming alliances, countries can pool their resources, share intelligence, and coordinate their military strategies to deter aggressive actions that threaten peace. This collaborative approach not only enhances national security but also fosters trust and mutual understanding among member states.

One of the primary functions of alliances is to create a sense of predictability in international relations. When nations commit to mutual defence agreements, they signal their willingness to support one another in times of crisis. This assurance can deter potential aggressors, as the costs of attacking an allied nation become significantly higher. As a result, alliances contribute to a more stable international environment, where nations are less likely to resort to unilateral military actions. This predictability is essential for maintaining order, as it allows countries to focus on diplomacy and cooperation rather than conflict.

In addition to enhancing security, alliances also play a vital role in promoting adherence to international law. Strong alliances encourage member states to uphold their commitments to treaties and agreements, reinforcing the principles of the global legal framework. By fostering a culture of compliance, alliances help create an environment where disputes can be resolved peacefully, reducing the likelihood of escalation into armed conflict. This commitment to the rule of law is essential for building a credible world order, as it demonstrates that nations can work together to uphold shared values and standards.

Globalisation has further emphasised the importance of alliances in maintaining order. As nations become more interdependent, the challenges they face often transcend borders, requiring collective action. Issues such as climate change, terrorism, and pandemics cannot be addressed in isolation, and alliances provide the necessary platform for coordinated responses. By working together through alliances, countries can leverage their collective strengths to tackle these global challenges, ultimately contributing to a more stable and secure world.

Finally, the influence of emerging technologies on international relations underscores the need for robust alliances. As new technologies reshape the geopolitical landscape, alliances must adapt to address the complexities of cyber threats, misinformation, and the proliferation of advanced weaponry. By collaborating on technological advancements and sharing best practices, allied nations can enhance their resilience and ensure that they remain prepared for future challenges. In this context, the function of alliances extends beyond traditional military cooperation, encompassing a broader commitment to safeguarding global order and promoting peace.

The risks and benefits of military cooperation

Military cooperation among nations serves as a double-edged sword, presenting both significant benefits and notable risks. On one hand, collaborative military efforts can enhance collective security, deter aggression, and strengthen alliances, which are crucial components for a stable and credible world order. Through joint exercises, intelligence sharing, and coordinated responses to threats, nations can build trust and foster deeper relationships. This trust is essential in a world where the complexity of international relations demands a united front against common threats, such as terrorism, cyber warfare, and regional conflicts.

The reliance on alliances may lead to entanglements in conflicts that do not directly serve a nation's interests, potentially dragging countries into wars that could have been avoided. Moreover, military cooperation can sometimes exacerbate tensions, especially if perceived as a threat by non-aligned nations. This perception can lead to an arms race or increased hostilities, undermining the very stability that military alliances aim to create. It is crucial for nations to navigate these waters carefully, ensuring that their partnerships are transparent and built on mutual understanding.

Another vital aspect of military cooperation is its relationship with international law. As nations collaborate militarily, they must align their actions with established legal frameworks to maintain legitimacy and prevent violations that could erode trust. Compliance with international law not only bolsters a nation's credibility but also reinforces a rules-based order that is essential for global peace. When military cooperation is grounded in legal principles, it can promote stability and foster a sense of accountability among nations, further enhancing cooperation in various domains beyond the military.

The impact of globalisation on national sovereignty also plays a significant role in military cooperation. As nations become more interconnected, the need for collaborative defence strategies grows. Global challenges such as climate change, pandemics, and economic instability demand a collective approach, where military cooperation may be necessary to address these multifaceted issues. While some may view this as a compromise of sovereignty, it can also be an opportunity for nations to gain collective strength, ensuring that they can respond effectively to challenges that transcend borders.

In conclusion, the relationship between military cooperation and a credible world order is intricate and multifaceted. While the potential benefits of enhanced security, trust, and collective action are clear, the risks associated with entanglements and compliance with international law must be carefully managed. As nations work together in an increasingly globalised world, fostering dialogue, understanding, and adherence to legal frameworks will be essential in building a credible and sustainable world order. Through thoughtful military cooperation, nations can navigate the complexities of international relations and contribute to a more peaceful and stable global environment.

Chapter 6: Non-state actors in world order

The rise of non-state influence

The rise of non-state influence is reshaping the contours of global governance and international relations, presenting both challenges and opportunities for a credible world order. In recent decades, the emergence of non-state actors such as multinational corporations, non-governmental organisations, and grassroots movements has altered traditional dynamics, shifting power away from solely nation-state actors. This evolution encourages us to reevaluate our understanding of sovereignty and authority in a world increasingly characterised by interconnectedness and interdependence.

Non-state actors often fill gaps left by national governments, providing humanitarian assistance, fostering dialogue, and advocating for social justice. Their ability to mobilise resources and influence public opinion can challenge established norms and push for reforms that support a more equitable global order. By engaging with these entities, nations can harness their expertise and networks to address pressing global issues, from climate change to human rights, thereby enhancing the credibility of international law and norms that underpin a stable world order.

Chapter 7: Multilateralism in a fractured world

Challenges facing multilateral institutions
    The challenges facing multilateral institutions are numerous and complex, yet they present an opportunity for nations to come together and build a more credible world order. As globalisation continues to reshape the landscape of international relations, multilateral institutions often find themselves struggling to adapt to rapid changes. The rise of nationalism in various countries has led to scepticism about the effectiveness and relevance of these institutions, making it crucial for nations to reaffirm their commitment to collaborative solutions that transcend individual interests. This moment calls for a renewed focus on the values that underpin multilateralism, emphasising cooperation and mutual benefit.

Paths toward effective multilateral cooperation

In an increasingly interconnected world, effective multilateral cooperation stands as a cornerstone for establishing a credible world order. Nations must recognize that collaboration is not merely an option but a necessity. The complexities of global challenges—ranging from climate change to pandemics—demand collective action. By fostering dialogue and understanding among diverse nations, we can build a foundation where mutual interests align. This approach not only strengthens diplomatic ties but also enhances the credibility of international institutions, which are crucial for addressing issues that transcend borders.

Chapter 8: Historical perspectives on world order

Lessons from the past

Understanding the evolution of world orders throughout history provides valuable insights into the necessity of building a credible global framework. Various civilisations have risen and fallen, each time shaping the political landscape in ways that offer important lessons for contemporary societies. For instance, the Treaty of Westphalia in 1648 established key principles of state sovereignty and non-interference, which still serve as foundational elements in international relations today. By examining these historical precedents, we recognise the importance of adhering to established norms and fostering cooperation among nations to mitigate conflicts and promote peace.

The role of international law has been pivotal in guiding interactions between states, and its evolution reveals the necessity for a credible world order. Historical milestones, such as the establishment of the United Nations and the adoption of the Universal Declaration of Human Rights, illustrate how collective efforts can create frameworks that uphold justice and accountability. Learning from the past, nations today must commit to strengthening international law to address emerging challenges, such as human rights violations and environmental crises. By doing so, they create a foundation of trust that enhances cooperation and fosters a stable global environment.

Adapting historical insights for the future

Historical insights provide a valuable lens through which we can address contemporary challenges and shape a credible world order for the future. By examining past world orders and their rise and fall, we can extract lessons that inform our current strategies for building trust among nations. The experiences of previous empires, alliances, and conflicts remind us that collaboration, respect for international law, and a commitment to shared values are essential for lasting peace. As we seek to adapt these lessons, we must recognise the importance of fostering a global environment in which nations can coexist harmoniously.

Chapter 9: Introduction to superpower credibility

Defining superpower credibility involves understanding the complex interplay between military strength, diplomatic influence, and the moral authority a nation wields in the international arena. Credibility is not merely a function of a superpower's military capabilities or economic resources; it also encompasses the perceived reliability and intentions of a nation when it engages in peacekeeping initiatives. In recent years, the actions of established superpowers have often raised questions about their true commitment to maintaining global peace and stability, particularly in light of their historical failures and the consequences of their interventions.

The historical record of superpowers serving as peacekeepers is fraught with challenges and failures. Numerous peacekeeping missions led by superpowers have ended in disarray, undermining their status as reliable global arbiters. Events such as the United States' involvement in Vietnam and the Soviet Union's actions in Afghanistan serve as stark reminders of how military interventions can devolve into protracted conflicts rather than successful peacekeeping efforts. These failures have eroded trust in superpowers, leading many nations to question whether they can genuinely facilitate conflict resolution or whether their interventions are primarily self-serving.

Military interventions, often justified under the guise of maintaining global stability, have shown a paradoxical effect on the very peace they aim to secure. Rather than fostering long-term stability, these interventions frequently exacerbate existing tensions and create new conflicts. The aftermath of interventions in Iraq and Libya, for instance, illustrates how the initial military actions led to power vacuums and ongoing violence, ultimately undermining the credibility of the intervening superpowers. This pattern raises critical concerns about whether military might can effectively serve as a tool for peacekeeping or if it contributes to a cycle of instability.

Economic sanctions, frequently employed by superpowers as a means of conflict resolution, further complicate the narrative of credibility. While sanctions are intended to pressure governments into changing their behaviour, they often harm civilian populations more than the targeted regimes. This misalignment of intentions and outcomes has led to scepticism regarding the effectiveness of sanctions in promoting peace. In numerous cases, the imposition of sanctions has hardened nationalistic sentiments and entrenchment of regimes, demonstrating that superpowers may lack the nuanced understanding necessary for credible peace efforts.

Finally, the dynamics of superpower rivalries significantly influence multilateral peacekeeping efforts. Competing interests among superpowers can lead to fragmentation within international coalitions, resulting in ineffective or contradictory actions in conflict zones. When superpowers prioritise their geopolitical agendas over collaborative peacekeeping efforts, the prospects for resolving conflicts diminish. Unilateral actions taken by one superpower can provoke backlash and escalate tensions, illustrating the precarious nature of international relations in an era marked by rivalry rather than cooperation. Ultimately, the credibility of superpowers as peacekeepers is undermined by their historical actions and the complexities of global politics, challenging their role in fostering a stable world order.

The role of peacekeeping in global stability

The role of peacekeeping in global stability has been a critical focus for international relations, particularly in the context of superpowers and their ability to maintain peace. Peacekeeping missions, often led by international organisations such as the United Nations, aim to provide a buffer in conflict zones, facilitate dialogue between warring parties, and support the establishment of sustainable governance structures. However, the effectiveness of these missions is often undermined by the very nations that position themselves as global peacekeepers. Current superpowers, despite their military capabilities and resources, frequently fail to qualify as credible peacekeepers due to their self-interested motives and historical patterns of intervention.

The impact of military intervention on global stability often exacerbates existing tensions rather than alleviating them. Superpower interventions are sometimes seen as acts of aggression rather than genuine peacekeeping efforts, leading to resentment and resistance from local populations. For instance, military actions in Iraq and Libya, marketed as necessary for stability, culminated in chaos and protracted conflict, demonstrating that intervention can destabilise regions rather than foster peace. This reality poses significant challenges for peacekeeping missions, as the legacy of military interventions can diminish local trust in international efforts and complicate future diplomatic engagements.

Chapter 10: Why current superpowers cannot qualify as credible world peacekeepers

The evolution of peacekeeping roles

The evolution of peacekeeping roles has been shaped significantly by the actions and policies of superpowers throughout history. Initially, peacekeeping missions emerged as a response to the aftermath of World War II, driven by the desire to maintain stability in conflict-ridden regions. Early efforts, often spearheaded by the United Nations, focused on observing ceasefires and facilitating dialogue among conflicting parties. However, as the geopolitical landscape evolved, so too did the expectations and responsibilities placed upon peacekeepers. The transition from traditional peacekeeping to more complex multidimensional missions reflected the changing nature of conflicts, which increasingly involved not only military but also humanitarian and political dimensions.

Superpowers have frequently positioned themselves as the leading actors in peacekeeping, yet their credibility has been undermined by historical failures. Numerous missions led or supported by superpowers have faltered due to a lack of genuine commitment to the principles of neutrality and impartiality. For instance, the U.S.-led interventions in the former Yugoslavia and Iraq were marked by significant challenges, including accusations of bias and the prioritisation of national interests over peacebuilding objectives. These failures not only diminished the effectiveness of peacekeeping missions but also fostered scepticism among local populations towards external intervention, complicating future efforts at conflict resolution.

Economic sanctions have been another tool employed by superpowers in the pursuit of conflict resolution, yet their effectiveness remains debatable. While sanctions are often intended to pressure regimes into compliance with international norms, they can also lead to humanitarian crises that disproportionately affect civilian populations. The long-standing sanctions against countries like Iran and North Korea illustrate how these measures can entrench adversarial relations rather than foster dialogue or peace. Consequently, the reliance on economic sanctions as a substitute for genuine diplomatic engagement raises concerns about the long-term viability of superpower-led peacekeeping efforts.

Superpower rivalries significantly influence the landscape of multilateral peacekeeping, often undermining collective efforts. Competing interests among major powers can lead to a lack of consensus on intervention strategies, resulting in fragmented approaches to peacekeeping missions. This rivalry was evident during the Syrian conflict, where divergent objectives among superpowers complicated diplomatic initiatives and hindered effective peacekeeping. The consequences of unilateral actions, such as bypassing multilateral frameworks in favour of national interests, further erode the credibility of superpowers as peacekeepers. As the international community grapples with the complexities of contemporary conflicts, the evolution of peacekeeping roles must consider the limitations imposed by superpower dynamics and the imperative for a more collaborative approach to maintaining global peace and stability.

Misalignment of national interests and global needs

The misalignment of national interests and global needs has become a defining characteristic of the actions taken by modern superpowers, significantly undermining their credibility as peacekeepers. As nations prioritise their own strategic agendas over collective global welfare, the ability to address pressing international issues diminishes. This disconnect is evident in various scenarios where superpowers have intervened in conflicts primarily to secure resources, enhance their geopolitical standing, or counter rivals, rather than to foster genuine peace and stability. Consequently, their interventions often exacerbate tensions rather than resolve them, leading to a cycle of violence and distrust among nations.

Interventions in the Middle East, such as the U.S. involvement in Iraq, have often been justified on the grounds of promoting democracy or combating terrorism. However, the aftermath has revealed a stark reality where local power vacuums and sectarian violence have replaced the anticipated peace. These failures highlight how national interests can cloud judgment, leading

27

superpowers to overlook the complexities of local dynamics and the importance of inclusive dialogue. As a result, the credibility of these nations as peacekeepers is significantly compromised, with many nations viewing them with scepticism rather than trust.

When superpowers engage in military actions without a clear understanding of the broader implications, the consequences can be devastating. For instance, interventions in Libya and Afghanistan, initially aimed at stabilising these regions, have often resulted in prolonged conflict and humanitarian crises. Such outcomes not only destabilise the regions directly involved but also have ripple effects that can destabilise neighbouring countries and alter global security dynamics. This pattern reinforces the perception that superpowers are more interested in exerting influence than in establishing lasting peace, further eroding their legitimacy on the global stage.

Finally, superpower rivalries complicate multilateral peacekeeping efforts by prioritizing national agendas over collaborative solutions. The ongoing tensions between major powers often lead to a fragmented international response to crises, as nations align themselves with competing blocs rather than working collectively. This factionalism can hinder the effectiveness of peacekeeping missions, as coordination and cooperation become challenging under such circumstances. Unilateral actions taken by superpowers, driven by their strategic interests, further entrench divisions and diminish the prospects for effective multilateral engagement. The result is a landscape where peacekeeping efforts falter, and global stability remains elusive, undermining the very foundations of international cooperation.

Perception vs. reality in superpower actions

Perception and reality often diverge significantly in the realm of international relations, particularly concerning the actions of superpowers. While these nations project an image of being peacekeepers, their real motives and the outcomes of their interventions often tell a different story. The public perception is frequently shaped by media narratives that highlight humanitarian efforts and peacekeeping missions, overshadowing the underlying political and economic agendas that guide these superpowers. This discrepancy not only affects how the world views these actions but also influences the legitimacy and effectiveness of superpower involvement in global peacekeeping.

Interventions in countries like Somalia and Iraq have been criticised for exacerbating conflicts rather than resolving them. In Somalia, the U.S.-led intervention in the early 1990s aimed to alleviate famine and restore order but resulted in a protracted civil war and a humanitarian crisis that continues to this day. Similarly, the invasion of Iraq in 2003, justified under the pretext of establishing democracy, led to significant instability in the region, with repercussions that are still felt across the Middle East. Such historical failures highlight the gap between the intended outcomes of superpower actions and the complex realities on the ground.

The impact of military interventions on global stability is another crucial aspect of this discussion. While superpowers often justify their military actions as necessary for maintaining peace, the aftermath frequently reveals a different narrative. Interventions can lead to power vacuums, civil unrest, and the rise of extremist groups, further destabilising regions rather than fostering peace. For instance, the military actions in Libya in 2011, aimed at overthrowing a dictatorial regime, resulted in chaos and ongoing conflict, raising questions about the responsibility of superpowers in creating a sustainable peace. This pattern illustrates that military might does not equate to effective peacekeeping, as the consequences of intervention can often be more destructive than the conflicts they seek to resolve.

Economic sanctions are another tool commonly employed by superpowers in their quest for conflict resolution. While they are often perceived as a non-military approach to compel nations to change their behaviour, the reality is that sanctions can have devastating effects on civilian populations, leading to humanitarian crises without necessarily achieving the desired political outcomes. The sanctions imposed on countries like Iran and North Korea, intended to curb nuclear ambitions, have led to widespread suffering among ordinary citizens, raising ethical questions about the efficacy and morality of such measures. This disconnect between the perception of sanctions as peaceful diplomacy and their harsh realities further complicates the credibility of superpowers in their role as peacekeepers.

Chapter 11: Historical failures of superpowers in peacekeeping missions

Case Study: The United States in Vietnam

The Vietnam War serves as a poignant case study in examining the credibility of superpowers as peacekeepers. The United States, motivated by the desire to contain communism, escalated its military presence in Vietnam in the 1960s, eventually committing hundreds of thousands of troops. This intervention, framed as a necessary measure to uphold democracy and prevent the spread of communism, instead resulted in a protracted conflict that questioned the moral and ethical foundations of U.S. foreign policy. The war's devastating impact on the Vietnamese population and landscape, alongside significant American casualties, led to widespread protest and scepticism regarding the U.S. role as a peacekeeper.

Despite significant military resources and technology, the U.S. struggled to secure a decisive victory against North Vietnamese forces and the Viet Cong. This lack of success undermined the U.S. credibility on the global stage, as it became clear that military might alone could not achieve the promised objectives of stability and democracy. The inability to effectively address the nuances of Vietnamese society, culture, and politics illustrated a critical gap in understanding that often plagues superpower interventions.

The impact of military intervention on global stability is starkly illustrated by the Vietnam War. The conflict not only destabilised Vietnam but also had far-reaching effects on neighbouring countries, leading to regional tensions and conflicts. The U.S. approach, characterised by heavy bombing campaigns and ground troop deployments, often resulted in collateral damage that bred resentment and unrest. This cycle of violence demonstrated that military intervention could exacerbate existing conflicts rather than resolve them, raising questions about the efficacy of superpowers in fostering long-term peace and stability.

Lastly, the unilateral actions taken by the U.S. in Vietnam showcase the consequences of a superpower acting without multilateral support. The war was marked by a lack of consensus among international allies and partners, leading to perceptions of American unilateralism. This isolation weakened the U.S. position and diminished its ability to act as a credible peacekeeper in the eyes of the international community. The lessons learned from Vietnam emphasise the necessity for superpowers to engage in cooperative, multilateral approaches to conflict resolution, recognising that their credibility as peacekeepers hinges on collaboration rather than unilateral actions.

Case Study: The Soviet Union in Afghanistan

The Soviet Union's intervention in Afghanistan from 1979 to 1989 serves as a critical case study in understanding the limitations of superpower credibility in peacekeeping efforts. The initial motivation behind the Soviet invasion was to support a communist government facing an insurgency from various factions, including the Mujahideen, who sought to overthrow the regime. The Soviet leadership believed that by deploying its military, it could stabilise the region and prevent the spread of Islamic fundamentalism, which they viewed as a threat to their own national security. However, the reality of the intervention quickly contradicted these intentions, revealing the complexities of military engagement in foreign conflicts.

As the Soviet forces became entrenched in Afghanistan, they faced fierce resistance from the Mujahideen, who were bolstered by external support from countries such as the United States, Pakistan, and Saudi Arabia. This external backing not only intensified the conflict but also turned the Soviet Union's intervention into a protracted war of attrition. The inability of the Soviet military to effectively quell the insurgency highlighted the fundamental flaw in the superpower's approach: reliance on military force without a comprehensive understanding of the local political and cultural dynamics. This miscalculation led to significant losses and ultimately contributed to the unravelling of Soviet credibility on the global stage.

The impact of the Soviet invasion extended beyond Afghanistan, affecting global stability and geopolitical relations. The war became a focal point in the Cold War, exacerbating tensions between the United States and the Soviet

Union. The U.S. framed the conflict as a battle between freedom and oppression, using it to rally support for anti-Soviet efforts worldwide. Consequently, the Soviet Union's failure in Afghanistan not only diminished its influence in the region but also emboldened other nations to challenge its authority. This case illustrates how military interventions can spark wider international rivalries and undermine the potential for multilateral peacekeeping initiatives.

Moreover, the Soviet experience in Afghanistan reveals the limitations of economic sanctions as a tool for conflict resolution. While the global response to the invasion included various sanctions aimed at isolating the Soviet Union, these measures often had limited effectiveness in altering its military strategy. Instead, the sanctions contributed to a sense of siege mentality within the Soviet leadership, reinforcing their resolve to maintain a presence in Afghanistan despite mounting casualties and international condemnation. This scenario underscores the complexity of using economic measures to compel a superpower to withdraw from a conflict, particularly when national pride and geopolitical interests are at stake.

Ultimately, the Soviet Union's intervention in Afghanistan exemplifies the consequences of unilateral actions in international conflicts. The lack of a coordinated international response or support for a legitimate peacekeeping framework led to a situation where military engagement became the primary tool for addressing political instability. The aftermath of the Soviet withdrawal left Afghanistan in a state of turmoil, which continues to resonate in contemporary discussions about superpower credibility and the efficacy of peacekeeping missions. This case study serves as a cautionary tale for current and future superpowers, highlighting the necessity for a nuanced understanding of conflict resolution that prioritises diplomacy and multilateral cooperation over unilateral military action.

Lessons from the Balkans: NATO's involvement

NATO's involvement in the Balkans during the 1990s serves as a critical case study in understanding the complexities of superpower engagement in peacekeeping efforts. The disintegration of Yugoslavia led to a series of violent conflicts characterised by ethnic strife and humanitarian crises. NATO, initially established as a defensive alliance against the Soviet Union, was thrust into a new role, prompting a revaluation of its purpose and capabilities in crisis response. The military interventions in Bosnia and Kosovo illustrated both the potential and limitations of NATO as a peacekeeping entity, shedding light on broader themes regarding the credibility of superpowers in maintaining global peace.

In Bosnia, NATO's first significant military intervention came in 1995 after years of brutal conflict that saw the Srebrenica massacre and widespread ethnic cleansing. The Dayton Accords, facilitated by NATO's involvement, brought an end to the war but also highlighted the challenges of enforcing peace in a deeply fractured society. The operation demonstrated how military might could achieve a ceasefire, yet it also revealed the difficulty of establishing long-term stability in a region rife with historical grievances. This duality of NATO's role as both peace enforcer and power player raises questions about the effectiveness of military interventions as a tool for sustainable peace.

The subsequent intervention in Kosovo in 1999 further complicated NATO's peacekeeping narrative. The decision to conduct an air campaign without United Nations approval underscored the contentious nature of unilateral actions in international conflicts. While the intervention was framed as a necessary response to humanitarian crises, it also provoked debates about the legitimacy and legality of bypassing established international frameworks. The aftermath of the Kosovo War illustrated those military interventions, while sometimes effective in stopping immediate violence, often leave unresolved political issues that can lead to future instability, thereby challenging the notion of superpowers as credible peacekeepers.

Economic sanctions, frequently employed alongside military interventions, also played a crucial role in the Balkans. In the lead-up to the conflicts, sanctions were imposed on Serbia in an attempt to curb aggression. However, the effectiveness of these measures was mixed, often exacerbating the plight of civilians while failing to achieve their intended political outcomes. The lesson from this period is that economic sanctions alone cannot resolve deep-seated ethnic and nationalistic tensions. Rather, they may contribute to further alienation and resistance, complicating the peacekeeping landscape and highlighting the limitations of superpower strategies in fostering genuine reconciliation.

Finally, NATO's actions in the Balkans reflect the broader implications of superpower rivalries and their impact on multilateral peacekeeping efforts.

The differing perspectives of member states on intervention strategies often hindered a cohesive approach to peacekeeping in the region. The challenges faced by NATO in Bosnia and Kosovo serve as reminders that superpower credibility is contingent not only on military strength but also on the ability to navigate complex geopolitical landscapes and to forge consensus among diverse stakeholders. Ultimately, the lessons from the Balkans indicate that without a commitment to addressing underlying issues and fostering genuine dialogue, military interventions risk becoming mere power plays rather than effective peacekeeping missions.

Chapter 12: The impact of military intervention on global stability

Short-term gains vs. long-term consequences

Short-term gains in international relations often overshadow the potential long-term consequences of superpower actions. When a superpower intervenes in a conflict, whether through military force or economic sanctions, the immediate objective is typically to assert influence, stabilize a region, or protect national interests. However, these interventions frequently neglect the complexities of the local context and the potential for unintended repercussions. The short-lived successes may bolster a superpower's credibility in the eyes of its allies, but they can also sow the seeds of future instability, as local grievances and power dynamics are often ignored or exacerbated.

The historical record of superpowers engaging in peacekeeping missions reveals a pattern of failures that undermine their credibility as effective peacekeepers. For instance, interventions in Vietnam, Iraq, and Afghanistan initially aimed to achieve stability and contain perceived threats but ultimately resulted in prolonged conflict and humanitarian crises. These instances demonstrate that military might does not equate to the ability to foster lasting peace. While superpowers may claim success in the short term, the long-term consequences often include fractured societies, radicalisation, and a resurgence of conflict, which challenge their role as credible arbiters of peace.

The impact of military intervention on global stability further complicates the narrative of short-term gains versus long-term consequences. While military interventions can lead to the immediate cessation of hostilities, they frequently create power vacuums that allow extremist groups to flourish. This dynamic not only destabilises the affected region but also has far-reaching implications for global security. The rise of ISIS in the wake of the Iraq War serves as a stark reminder of how interventions, rather than resolving conflict, can lead to a cycle of violence that demands further military engagement, thus perpetuating a cycle of instability.

Case Studies: Iraq and Libya

The military interventions in Iraq and Libya serve as poignant examples of how superpowers often fail to act as credible peacekeepers. In Iraq, the invasion in 2003, led by the United States, was justified on the grounds of dismantling weapons of mass destruction and promoting democracy. However, the aftermath was characterised by prolonged instability, sectarian violence, and the emergence of extremist groups, most notably ISIS. The initial promise of liberation quickly devolved into chaos, undermining the credibility of the United States as a responsible actor on the global stage. This situation illustrates how the imposition of power without a comprehensive understanding of the local context can lead to disastrous consequences, casting doubt on the efficacy of superpower-led peacekeeping efforts.

In Libya, the 2011 intervention, which consisted of a NATO-led bombing campaign to protect civilians during the civil conflict, initially appeared to achieve its objectives. However, the subsequent power vacuum and lack of a coherent post-intervention strategy resulted in a fractured state plagued by militia violence and ongoing civil strife. The failure to establish a stable governance structure post-intervention not only undermined the initial humanitarian intent but also highlighted the dangers of unilateral military actions. As Libya devolved into chaos, the credibility of the intervening powers diminished further, showcasing the limitations of military intervention as a tool for achieving lasting peace.

In both Iraq and Libya, the interventions led to regional instability, affecting neighbouring countries and creating new challenges for international security. For instance, the instability in Libya has been linked to the rise of human trafficking networks and the spread of arms across the Mediterranean. Similarly, the repercussions of the Iraq War have reverberated throughout the Middle East, contributing to sectarian tensions and influencing geopolitical dynamics. These cases underscore how superpower interventions, rather than serving as stabilising forces, can exacerbate existing tensions and lead to broader regional conflicts.

Economic sanctions, often employed as a tool for conflict resolution, also reveal the limitations of superpower credibility. In the wake of the Iraq invasion, sanctions were placed on the country, which were intended to pressure the regime into compliance with international norms. However, these sanctions disproportionately affected the civilian population, leading to humanitarian crises without achieving the intended political outcomes. In Libya, sanctions were similarly utilised, but they often failed to address the underlying issues driving conflict. This raises critical questions about the effectiveness of economic measures as a means of fostering peace and highlights the moral dilemmas faced by superpowers when choosing how to intervene in complex international crises.

Superpower rivalries further complicate multilateral peacekeeping efforts, as seen in the contexts of Iraq and Libya. The competing interests of major powers often lead to fragmented approaches to conflict resolution, diminishing the effectiveness of collective action. In Iraq, the U.S. faced opposition from countries like Russia and Iran, which had their own agendas, complicating international consensus on peacekeeping strategies. In Libya, the involvement of various external actors with differing objectives has stymied efforts to establish a unified government and restore order. These rivalries not only impede the credibility of superpowers as peacekeepers but also perpetuate cycles of violence and instability, demonstrating the urgent need for a revaluation of how these powers engage in international conflicts.

The role of local dynamics in military interventions

The dynamics of local contexts play a crucial role in shaping the outcomes of military interventions by superpowers. Each conflict zone possesses its unique political, social, and cultural fabric that significantly influences the effectiveness of external military actions. While superpowers often approach interventions with a preconceived notion of imposing order or stability, they frequently overlook the complexities that define local realities. Understanding these dynamics is essential for evaluating the credibility of superpowers as peacekeepers. Ignoring the historical and sociopolitical intricacies can lead to misguided strategies that exacerbate rather than alleviate conflict.

Chapter 13: The Influence of economic sanctions on conflict resolution

The theory behind economic sanctions

Economic sanctions are a tool of foreign policy employed by countries to influence the behaviour of other nations without resorting to military intervention. The fundamental premise of economic sanctions is to apply economic pressure on a target state in order to compel it to change specific policies or behaviours that are deemed unacceptable by the sanctioning country. This mechanism operates on the belief that economic hardship will lead to political change, as affected nations may experience internal dissent, weakened governance, and diminished capacity to sustain their agendas. Although sanctions are often perceived as a less aggressive alternative to military action, their effectiveness in achieving diplomatic goals is a complex and contentious issue.

There are several theoretical frameworks that underpin the use of economic sanctions. One prominent theory is the "rational actor model," which posits that states, as rational entities, will respond to incentives and disincentives in a predictable manner. Sanctions are expected to create a cost-benefit analysis for the targeted state, prompting it to alter its behaviour in order to alleviate the economic burden. However, this model assumes that the targeted state will act in its own best interest, which may not always hold true. In some cases, governments may double down on their policies in the face of sanctions, viewing them as an affront to national sovereignty or as a rallying point for domestic support.

Another important aspect of sanctions theory is the distinction between "smart" sanctions and comprehensive sanctions. Smart sanctions are tailored measures that target specific individuals, entities, or sectors of the economy, aiming to minimise collateral damage to the general population. This approach is based on the understanding that widespread economic suffering can lead to humanitarian crises and may undermine the legitimacy of the sanctioning country. On the other hand, comprehensive sanctions often impose blanket restrictions that can exacerbate poverty and instability, potentially leading to unintended consequences such as increased support for authoritarian regimes or the rise of extremist groups.

The historical record of economic sanctions reveals a mixed bag of outcomes in terms of efficacy. While some sanctions have successfully achieved their intended goals—such as the sanctions against South Africa during the apartheid era—many others have faltered, failing to produce meaningful change or even backfiring. The case of Iraq in the 1990s illustrates the limitations of sanctions, as they resulted in significant humanitarian suffering without compelling the regime to comply with international demands. Such failures raise critical questions about the moral implications of using economic sanctions as a foreign policy tool and the responsibilities of sanctioning nations to minimise harm to civilian populations.

In the context of superpower rivalries, the use of economic sanctions can further complicate global stability and international relations. When major powers engage in sanctions as a means of exerting influence over weaker states, the potential for escalation increases, as affected nations may seek support from rival powers. This dynamic can erode multilateral efforts at peacekeeping and conflict resolution, as states become entrenched in their positions and less willing to cooperate in diplomatic negotiations. Ultimately, understanding the theory behind economic sanctions is essential for evaluating their role within the broader framework of international relations and assessing the credibility of superpowers as effective peacekeepers.

Case Studies: sanctions on Iran and North Korea

The imposition of sanctions on Iran and North Korea serves as a significant case study in understanding the limitations and contradictions of superpower credibility in peacekeeping efforts. Sanctions, which are often positioned as tools for promoting peace and stability, can frequently lead to unintended consequences that exacerbate tensions rather than alleviate them. In the case of Iran, the United States and its allies have employed a range of economic sanctions aimed at curtailing its nuclear program. While these measures were intended to compel compliance with international norms, they have also fostered a climate of hostility, leading Iran to double down on its nuclear ambitions and pursue aggressive regional policies.

Similarly, North Korea's experience with sanctions illustrates the challenges faced by superpowers in enforcing compliance and achieving diplomatic resolutions. The United Nations Security Council has imposed numerous sanctions in response to North Korea's nuclear tests and missile launches. However, these sanctions have not succeeded in denuclearising the regime; instead, they have reinforced its isolation and prompted North Korea to enhance its military capabilities. The regime utilises the sanctions narrative to rally domestic support, portraying itself as a victim of external aggression, which complicates the prospects for diplomatic engagement and peacekeeping.

In both Iran and North Korea, sanctions have led to shortages of essential goods and services, creating suffering for ordinary citizens while having little effect on the political elite. This disconnection raises critical ethical questions about the efficacy and morality of sanctions as a peacekeeping strategy. The inability of superpowers to target sanctions effectively without harming civilians undermines their credibility and casts doubt on their commitment to human rights and humanitarian principles.

Furthermore, the strategic rivalries among superpowers significantly influence the effectiveness of sanctions as a tool for conflict resolution. In the case of Iran, divisions between the U.S. and European allies on how to approach Iran's nuclear ambitions have weakened the cohesion necessary for a unified sanctions regime. Similarly, China's support for North Korea complicates international efforts to impose and enforce sanctions. These rivalries can lead to a lack of consensus on multilateral peacekeeping efforts, diluting the impact of sanctions and reducing the likelihood of successful diplomatic resolutions.

Evaluating effectiveness: successes and failures

Evaluating the effectiveness of superpowers in their roles as peacekeepers reveals a complex landscape of successes and failures that challenges the notion of their credibility. Historical analyses show that while superpowers have occasionally succeeded in mediating conflicts, their interventions often lack long-term effectiveness. For instance, the United States' involvement in peacekeeping efforts in the Balkans during the 1990s is cited as a relative success, showcasing the potential for a superpower to stabilise a region. However, these instances are overshadowed by numerous failures where interventions led to unintended consequences, such as exacerbating conflicts or creating power vacuums, as seen in Iraq post-2003.

Chapter 14: Superpower rivalries and their effect on multilateral peacekeeping

Historical context of superpower rivalries

The historical context of superpower rivalries provides a crucial framework for understanding the limitations of current superpowers as credible world peacekeepers. The 20th century, marked by the Cold War, showcased a stark dichotomy between the United States and the Soviet Union, each vying for global influence. This rivalry was characterised by a series of proxy wars, ideological confrontations, and arms races, which often undermined international peace efforts. The focus on military superiority and political dominance over cooperative diplomacy laid the groundwork for skepticism regarding the ability of superpowers to act as neutral peacekeepers.

The impact of military intervention on global stability cannot be understated. Superpowers, in their pursuit of geopolitical interests, have frequently overlooked the complex social and political dynamics of the regions they engage. This has resulted in fractured societies and protracted conflicts that endure long after military forces withdraw. The legacy of such interventions often includes a power vacuum, which can give rise to more severe instability, further complicating the prospects for peace. As these historical lessons reveal, the reliance on military might as a means of conflict resolution has proven ineffective, raising concerns about the credibility of superpowers in peacekeeping missions.

Case study: The cold war and its legacy

The Cold War, a period marked by intense geopolitical rivalry between the United States and the Soviet Union, serves as a critical case study in understanding the complexities of superpower credibility in peacekeeping. This era, spanning from the end of World War II to the early 1990s, was characterised by a series of proxy wars, military interventions, and a pervasive ideological struggle. The actions taken by these superpowers during this time highlight significant historical failures that raise questions about their ability to act as credible peacekeepers in contemporary conflicts. The Cold War's legacy continues to shape international relations, influencing current superpowers and their approaches to global peacekeeping.

Throughout the Cold War, both superpowers frequently engaged in military interventions under the guise of protecting democracy or countering communism. These interventions often resulted in significant humanitarian crises and long-lasting instability in affected regions. For instance, the U.S. involvement in Vietnam and the Soviet Union's actions in Afghanistan exemplify the detrimental impacts of military interventions driven by superpower agendas. Rather than fostering peace, these actions often exacerbated conflicts, leading to further violence and suffering. This history serves as a cautionary tale, illustrating that military might does not equate to effective peacekeeping and that superpowers often prioritise their strategic interests over genuine global stability.

Current Rivalries: US-China and its implications

The rivalry between the United States and China has emerged as one of the defining geopolitical dynamics of the 21st century. This competition is not merely a struggle for economic supremacy but extends to various realms, including military influence, technological advancement, and ideological dominance. As both nations vie for global leadership, their actions and policies significantly impact international relations and the overall stability of the global order. This rivalry raises questions about the ability of either superpower to act as a credible peacekeeper, given their preoccupation with national interests and strategic positioning.

The US, for instance, has frequently intervened in regions where its interests were at stake, leading to prolonged conflicts rather than resolution. China's rise, marked by initiatives such as the Belt and Road Initiative, reflects its ambition to expand its influence but also raises concerns about its commitment to global governance and peacekeeping. The historical failings of these superpowers in maintaining peace suggest that their current rivalry may exacerbate tensions rather than contribute to a collaborative approach towards global stability.

The US has often employed military force under the guise of humanitarian intervention, yet these actions have frequently resulted in unintended consequences, including prolonged instability and the rise of extremist groups. China's military assertiveness in the South China Sea and its support for authoritarian regimes demonstrate a willingness to prioritise national sovereignty over international norms, further complicating peacekeeping efforts. As both nations continue to elevate their military postures, the potential for conflict increases, undermining the possibility of effective peacekeeping on a multilateral scale.

The consequences of unilateral actions taken by superpowers have far-reaching implications for multilateral peacekeeping efforts. The US's withdrawal from international agreements, such as the Paris Climate Accord and the Iran nuclear deal, has weakened collective efforts to address global challenges. Similarly, China's increasing disregard for international norms in its territorial claims undermines the legitimacy of multilateral institutions. As these nations prioritise their rivalry over cooperation, the prospects for effective peacekeeping diminish, leaving smaller nations vulnerable to the repercussions of their actions. The ongoing US-China rivalry challenges the notion that superpowers can serve as reliable peacekeepers, emphasizing the need for a revaluation of their roles in fostering global peace and stability.

Chapter 15: The consequences of unilateral actions in international conflicts

Defining unilateralism in international relations
　　Unilateralism in international relations refers to the approach where a state acts independently without seeking the consent or cooperation of other states, especially in matters of foreign policy and military intervention. This approach often arises from a belief in the state's own capacity to achieve objectives without the need for multilateral frameworks or alliances. While unilateral actions can occasionally yield swift results, they frequently raise questions about legitimacy, efficacy, and the long-term consequences for global stability. Understanding unilateralism is crucial for evaluating the roles of contemporary superpowers and their credibility as peacekeepers in a world characterized by increasingly complex interdependencies.

　　Historically, the unilateral actions of superpowers have often undermined their roles as credible peacekeepers. Events such as the U.S. invasion of Iraq in 2003 serve as critical examples of how unilateral military interventions can lead to significant destabilisation in regions. Despite claims of promoting democracy and security, such actions frequently resulted in power vacuums, civil strife, and prolonged conflict, ultimately contradicting the stated objectives of peacekeeping. This historical precedent illustrates how the failure to engage with the international community can lead to disastrous outcomes, diminishing the superpower's credibility in subsequent peacekeeping efforts.

　　The impact of military intervention on global stability is another critical aspect of unilateralism. When a superpower opts for direct military action without multilateral support, it risks igniting further conflict and resentment among affected nations. This often leads to a cycle of violence where the initial intervention provokes retaliatory actions from local groups or rival states. Such dynamics not only challenge the immediate effectiveness of peacekeeping efforts but can also destabilise entire regions, as seen in the aftermath of various interventions in the Middle East and beyond. The consequences of unilateral military actions extend beyond the target nation, affecting global perceptions of legitimacy and trust in international governance structures.

Case Studies: US interventions in Syria and Afghanistan

The United States has engaged in military interventions in various contexts, with Syria and Afghanistan standing out as prominent case studies that illustrate the complexities and challenges of superpower involvement in peacekeeping. In Afghanistan, the U.S. initiated its intervention in response to the September 11 attacks, targeting the Taliban regime that harboured al-Qaeda. Initially framed as a mission to dismantle terrorism, the intervention quickly evolved into a prolonged conflict that lasted nearly two decades. Despite significant investments in military and economic resources, the U.S. struggled to establish a stable government, leading to a resurgence of the Taliban and raising questions about the long-term efficacy of military intervention as a strategy for peacekeeping.

In Syria, the U.S. response to the civil war that erupted in 2011 further exemplifies the difficulties of external intervention. Initially, the U.S. supported moderate rebel factions aiming to overthrow the Assad regime, viewing it as a means to promote democracy and stability in the region. However, the intervention became complicated as various factions emerged, including extremist groups like ISIS. The absence of a coherent strategy, combined with the involvement of other international actors, complicated the situation, leading to a stalemate and exacerbating humanitarian crises. This case highlights how military interventions often lack clear objectives and can result in unintended consequences, undermining the credibility of superpowers as peacekeepers.

The ripple effects on global governance

The dynamics of global governance have been significantly altered by the actions and inactions of current superpowers, leading to a complex interplay of credibility and authority in peacekeeping efforts. As these nations engage in various forms of intervention, the repercussions extend beyond immediate military outcomes, affecting international norms, diplomatic relations, and the overall stability of regions involved. The perceived credibility of superpowers as peacekeepers is increasingly questioned, particularly when their interventions are viewed as self-serving rather than altruistic. This skepticism undermines their ability to act as effective arbiters in global conflicts, resulting in a ripple effect that challenges the foundations of international governance.

Chapter 16: Rethinking the role of superpowers in peacekeeping

Alternatives to traditional peacekeeping

Alternatives to traditional peacekeeping have become a pressing subject of discussion in the context of global stability and the effectiveness of superpower involvement. As traditional peacekeeping often relies on military forces deployed by superpowers, the limitations and failures of these approaches have prompted exploration of alternative methods. These alternatives encompass a range of strategies, including regional peacekeeping efforts, mediation initiatives by non-state actors, and the rise of community-based conflict resolution mechanisms. Each of these alternatives presents distinct advantages that can enhance the credibility and effectiveness of peacekeeping efforts compared to traditional superpower-led missions.

Regional peacekeeping efforts have emerged as a significant alternative, allowing countries closer to the conflict zone to take the lead. Such initiatives often benefit from a deeper understanding of the local context, culture, and historical grievances that may not be apparent to outside superpowers. For instance, organisations like the African Union and the Economic Community of West African States have successfully deployed peacekeeping missions in various African conflicts, demonstrating that regional actors can often navigate complex local dynamics more effectively than distant superpowers. This localised approach can lead to more sustainable peace, as it fosters ownership of the peace process among the affected populations.

Mediation initiatives led by non-state actors, including NGOs and community leaders, also provide a viable alternative to traditional peacekeeping. These actors often have established trust within communities and can facilitate dialogue between conflicting parties in a way that external forces cannot. By emphasising grassroots involvement, these initiatives can address the underlying issues of conflict, such as economic disparities and social injustices. Furthermore, non-state actors can mobilise resources and support from a variety of stakeholders, creating a comprehensive network for peacebuilding that transcends the limitations of superpower influence.

Community-based conflict resolution mechanisms are gaining traction as effective alternatives to conventional peacekeeping. These approaches empower local populations to take active roles in resolving disputes and reconciling differences, thereby fostering a sense of agency and responsibility. Local councils, traditional leaders, and civil society organisations have proven effective in mediating conflicts by drawing on indigenous practices and cultural norms, which can resonate more with the affected communities than imposed solutions from superpowers. This bottom-up approach not only enhances the legitimacy of the peace process but also contributes to long-term stability by reinforcing social cohesion.

Despite the challenges inherent in these alternative peacekeeping methods, their potential to complement or even replace traditional superpower interventions is significant. The historical failures of superpowers in peacekeeping missions, marked by an often-unilateral approach and a lack of genuine commitment to long-term peace, highlight the need for diverse strategies. By embracing regional and non-state mediation, as well as community-led initiatives, the international community can work toward a more inclusive and effective peacekeeping framework. Ultimately, these alternatives may offer the credibility and local legitimacy that are frequently lacking in superpower-led efforts, paving the way for a more stable and peaceful global landscape.

The importance of multilateral approaches

The importance of multilateral approaches in addressing global conflicts cannot be overstated, particularly in a world where superpowers often fail to act as credible peacekeepers. Historically, superpowers have pursued unilateral strategies that prioritise their own interests over collaborative solutions. This approach has led to numerous failures in peacekeeping missions, where the lack of broad-based support often undermined the legitimacy and effectiveness of interventions. In contrast, multilateral approaches facilitate greater cooperation among nations, pooling resources, expertise, and perspectives to develop more comprehensive solutions to complex conflicts.

When multiple countries and organizations participate in a mission, it reflects a collective commitment to peace that transcends national interests. This collective action can foster trust and cooperation among conflicting parties, as they perceive the involvement of diverse stakeholders as a sign of impartiality. For instance, missions led by the United Nations or regional coalitions often carry the weight of international consensus, which can help mitigate hostilities and create an environment conducive to negotiation and reconciliation.

Moreover, multilateral approaches allow for a more holistic understanding of conflicts. Different nations bring unique experiences and insights that can inform more effective strategies for conflict resolution. Superpowers, often driven by their geopolitical agendas, may overlook critical local dynamics or historical grievances that contribute to conflict. In multilateral settings, the inclusion of various perspectives can lead to more nuanced solutions that address the root causes of disputes rather than merely the symptoms.

Future directions for global peacekeeping efforts

To address the shortcomings of current superpowers in global peacekeeping, it is essential to explore alternative frameworks for international cooperation. As traditional peacekeeping efforts often falter due to the vested interests of superpowers, a more inclusive approach that prioritises multilateral engagement is necessary. This could involve strengthening regional organisations, such as the African Union or the Association of Southeast Asian Nations, which may possess a more nuanced understanding of local conflicts and cultural dynamics.

Economic sanctions have also been a cornerstone of superpower strategies in conflict resolution, yet their effectiveness remains contentious. Often, sanctions disproportionately affect civilian populations and can entrench adversarial positions. Future peacekeeping efforts should explore alternative economic measures that encourage cooperation rather than punishment. Approaches such as targeted sanctions that focus on specific individuals or entities, along with incentives for compliance, can provide a more balanced framework for addressing conflicts. Additionally, fostering economic development in post-conflict regions can help mitigate the conditions that foster violence and instability.

Lastly, the dynamics of superpower rivalries significantly influence multilateral peacekeeping efforts. Competition among superpowers often leads to fragmented international responses to crises, undermining collective action. Moving forward, it is essential to establish mechanisms that promote transparency and collaboration among nations, reducing the likelihood of unilateral actions that can escalate tensions. Initiatives that encourage joint peacekeeping missions and shared responsibilities can cultivate a spirit of cooperation. By reframing the narrative around global peacekeeping from one dominated by superpower interests to one rooted in collective security, the international community can work towards more effective and credible peacekeeping efforts.

Chapter 17: Conclusion: The path forward for credible peacekeeping

Summary of Key Findings

The examination of superpower credibility as peacekeepers reveals a consistent pattern of shortcomings that undermines their effectiveness in global peacekeeping efforts. Current superpowers, despite their immense military and economic resources, often struggle to maintain impartiality and legitimacy in international conflicts. Their historical involvement in peacekeeping missions frequently demonstrates a prioritization of national interests over genuine peace and stability, leading to outcomes that not only fail to resolve conflicts but may exacerbate them. This persistent failure calls into question the ability of these nations to act as credible mediators in global crises.

RECOMMENDATIONS FOR superpowers

Superpowers, despite their significant resources and influence, often fall short of being credible world peacekeepers. To enhance their effectiveness in this role, it is essential for them to adopt a more collaborative approach in international relations. One key recommendation is the establishment of multilateral frameworks that prioritise collective security over unilateral actions. By engaging with a diverse range of nations, superpowers can foster trust and legitimacy in peacekeeping efforts, ensuring that interventions are viewed as collective endeavours rather than self-serving missions. This shift in strategy can mitigate accusations of imperialism and enhance the credibility of superpowers in global governance.

The role of non-state actors in peacekeeping

Non-state actors have increasingly become significant players in the realm of peacekeeping, often filling gaps left by traditional state-centric approaches.

These entities, which include non-governmental organisations (NGOs), community-based groups, and influential individuals, can operate where state actors may be unwilling or unable to act effectively. By leveraging their local knowledge, humanitarian focus, and often more flexible operational frameworks, non-state actors contribute to peacebuilding initiatives that aim to resolve conflicts and foster stability. Their involvement can complement official peacekeeping missions, providing essential services and support while advocating for marginalised communities caught in the crossfire of violence.

Chapter 18: Understanding the priceless value of world Peace

Defining world peace

Defining world peace involves understanding it as more than just the absence of conflict; it encompasses a comprehensive state of harmony among nations, communities, and individuals. It signifies a world where justice prevails, human rights are respected, and the rule of law is upheld. In this context, world peace is intrinsically linked to social, economic, and environmental factors, suggesting that a peaceful society is one where equitable access to resources and opportunities exists. This broader definition highlights the interconnectedness of various aspects of human life and emphasises that peace is a multifaceted goal that requires collective action and commitment.

When nations experience peace, they can redirect resources from military expenditures to social programs, infrastructure development, and education, fostering sustainable economic growth. Peaceful societies attract foreign investments and promote trade, leading to job creation and improved living standards. Conversely, regions plagued by conflict often suffer from economic stagnation, decreased productivity, and increased poverty levels. By investing in peace initiatives, countries can create a stable environment conducive to economic prosperity, illustrating that the value of world peace extends beyond moral considerations to tangible economic advantages.

The psychological impacts of peace on individual well-being cannot be overstated. Living in a peaceful environment reduces stress, anxiety, and fear, allowing individuals to thrive emotionally and mentally. Peace fosters a sense of security and belonging, which is essential for personal development and societal cohesion. Research indicates that communities characterised by peace report higher levels of happiness and life satisfaction. Furthermore, peaceful societies cultivate resilience and social capital, enabling individuals to cope better with challenges and adversities. Thus, promoting world peace is not merely a strategic goal but a vital necessity for enhancing the quality of life for individuals globally.

Environmental sustainability is another critical aspect of peaceful societies. Conflict often leads to environmental degradation as natural resources are exploited or destroyed in the pursuit of power and control. In contrast, peaceful communities are more likely to implement policies that prioritise sustainable practices and conservation efforts. A stable environment fosters cooperation in managing shared resources, such as water and forests, and encourages collaborative efforts to combat climate change. By emphasising peace, societies can create a foundation for environmental stewardship, highlighting the intrinsic link between global stability and ecological well-being.

Education plays a crucial role in promoting world peace by instilling values of tolerance, empathy, and critical thinking in future generations. Educational initiatives focused on peacebuilding empower young people to engage in dialogue, resolve conflicts amicably, and embrace diversity. Historical case studies demonstrate that societies that prioritize education and inclusivity tend to experience greater stability and prosperity. Furthermore, youth engagement in peace initiatives is vital, as young people possess the potential to drive social change and innovation. By leveraging technology and fostering global dialogue, educational institutions can cultivate a culture of peace, ensuring that the pursuit of world peace remains a collective responsibility that transcends borders and generations.

Historical Perspectives on Peace

Historical perspectives on peace reveal the evolving understanding of its significance and the multifaceted benefits it brings to societies. Throughout history, various cultures and civilisations have grappled with the concept of peace, often recognising its crucial role in fostering stability and prosperity. Ancient texts and practices from diverse regions, such as the teachings of Confucius in China, the philosophies of the Greeks, and the peace treaties of indigenous tribes, reflect a long-standing acknowledgment of peace as a foundational element for societal advancement. These historical insights provide valuable lessons about the importance of sustained peace in achieving collective goals and the interdependence of nations.

The economic benefits of global stability and peace have been apparent throughout history. Regions that have experienced prolonged periods of peace, such as post-World War II Europe, have seen significant economic growth and development. The Marshall Plan, which aimed to rebuild war-torn European economies, illustrates how peace can catalyse economic recovery and cooperation. In contrast, countries embroiled in conflict often suffer from stagnation, resource depletion, and increased poverty. Historical case studies show that nations investing in peace initiatives tend to experience economic dividends, as stability attracts investment, fosters trade, and encourages innovation.

The psychological impacts of peace on individual well-being are well documented in historical contexts. During periods of conflict, communities often experience trauma, loss, and disconnection, leading to widespread mental health issues. Conversely, societies that prioritise peace tend to foster environments conducive to emotional and psychological healing. Historical accounts from societies that have undergone reconciliation processes, such as South Africa post-apartheid, showcase the importance of peace in promoting mental well-being and community cohesion. These examples highlight how peace not only benefits individuals but also strengthens societal bonds and resilience.

Environmental sustainability is another critical dimension historically linked to peaceful societies. Many indigenous cultures have demonstrated a harmonious relationship with nature, emphasising stewardship and sustainability as core values. Throughout history, conflict has often led to environmental degradation, resource exploitation, and loss of biodiversity. In contrast, peaceful societies tend to prioritise sustainable practices, fostering a balance between human activity and ecological preservation. Historical examples, such as the practices of the indigenous peoples of North America, reveal that peace can facilitate a deeper commitment to environmental conservation and sustainability.

Finally, the role of education in promoting world peace has been recognized across various historical epochs. Educational initiatives aimed at fostering understanding, tolerance, and conflict resolution have played a significant role in peacebuilding efforts. Historical movements advocating for universal education, such as the Enlightenment, have underscored the belief that informed citizens are essential for achieving lasting peace. By examining the historical evolution of educational practices and their impact on peace initiatives, we can better appreciate the importance of fostering a culture of peace through learning and dialogue. This understanding is vital for engaging youth and promoting innovative approaches to peace in contemporary society.

The philosophical debate on the value of world peace

The philosophical debate on the value of peace has engaged thinkers for centuries, exploring the fundamental nature of peace itself and its profound implications for human existence. At its core, the discussion revolves around the intrinsic worth of peace compared to the tangible benefits it can bring. While some argue that peace is a mere absence of conflict, others contend that true peace encompasses a state of harmony characterised by justice, equality, and cooperation. This nuanced understanding challenges us to consider peace not only as a goal but as a vital framework for human flourishing, influencing economic stability, social cohesion, and overall well-being.

Economically, the value of peace is often illustrated through the concept of stability. Nations that experience prolonged periods of peace tend to enjoy robust economic growth, as resources are diverted from military expenditures toward social and infrastructural development. Historical case studies reveal that countries emerging from conflict frequently face significant challenges in rebuilding their economies, whereas those that maintain peaceful relations can foster environments conducive to investment and innovation. The correlation between peace and economic prosperity highlights how the costs associated with conflict far outweigh the benefits of war, making a compelling case for prioritizing global peace initiatives.

Chapter 19: Peace as a catalyst for economic growth

Peace serves as a fundamental catalyst for economic growth, creating a conducive environment for investment, development, and innovation. When societies experience stability, they attract both domestic and foreign investments, which are critical for economic advancement. Investors seek reliable markets where the risk of disruption is minimal. In peaceful settings, businesses can operate efficiently, allowing for the optimal allocation of resources and fostering an atmosphere of trust and collaboration. Consequently, a nation marked by peace often sees increased economic activity, job creation, and overall prosperity.

The connection between peace and economic growth is also evident in the social fabric of a community. Peaceful societies tend to prioritise education, healthcare, and infrastructure, all of which are essential components of a thriving economy. When governments can allocate their resources toward development rather than conflict resolution, citizens benefit from improved social services and opportunities for personal advancement. Access to quality education and healthcare not only enhances individual well-being but also boosts productivity, creating a positive feedback loop that further stimulates economic growth.

Moreover, the psychological impacts of peace on individual well-being can lead to significant economic benefits. Individuals in peaceful environments report higher levels of life satisfaction and lower incidences of stress-related illnesses. This psychological stability fosters creativity and innovation, which are vital for economic dynamism. When people feel secure, they are more likely to take risks, start businesses, and invest in their futures. The collective mental health of a population directly influences its economic performance, making peace an integral component of sustainable economic development.

Lastly, peacebuilding through international cooperation enhances economic growth on a global scale. Nations that collaborate on trade agreements, environmental initiatives, and humanitarian efforts create a web of interdependence that fosters stability. This interconnectedness not only facilitates the flow of goods and services but also encourages cultural exchange and mutual understanding. By prioritising peace and cooperation, countries can create an environment where economic growth is not just a national objective but a global endeavour, reinforcing the notion that peace is indeed priceless in its ability to drive prosperity for all.

The cost of conflict: Economic analysis

The economic implications of conflict are profound and multifaceted, extending far beyond immediate destruction to encompass long-term impacts on societies and nations. Armed conflicts disrupt trade, dismantle infrastructure, and divert resources away from essential services such as education and healthcare. The cost of war can be quantified not only in terms of military expenditure but also through lost opportunities for economic growth and social development. For instance, nations embroiled in conflict often experience a sharp decline in foreign investment, stifling entrepreneurship and innovation, which are critical for economic vitality.

Moreover, the ripple effects of conflict can destabilise entire regions, leading to increased poverty and unemployment rates. The displacement of populations due to violence creates a humanitarian crisis, straining resources in neighbouring countries and resulting in a loss of human capital. Refugees often face limited access to jobs, education, and healthcare, perpetuating cycles of poverty and disenfranchisement. The economic burden on host countries can be significant, as they grapple with the costs of providing for displaced individuals while trying to maintain stability and growth.

From a broader perspective, the economic analysis of conflict also considers the costs associated with rebuilding and recovery. Post-conflict reconstruction requires substantial investments in infrastructure, governance, and social services. These investments are often financed through international aid, which can lead to dependency and hinder self-sustaining growth. Additionally, the psychological toll of conflict can lead to long-term health issues, further burdening economies through increased healthcare costs and reduced productivity. Addressing the aftermath of violence is imperative not only for immediate recovery but also for fostering sustainable peace and development.

In contrast, the benefits of peace extend well beyond the absence of violence. Economic stability in peaceful societies fosters an environment conducive to investment, innovation, and job creation. Countries that prioritise peace tend to see improvements in their gross domestic product (GDP), as resources can be allocated toward development rather than conflict management. Furthermore, peaceful societies exhibit higher levels of human development, including education and healthcare outcomes, which are critical for fostering a skilled workforce and promoting overall economic growth.

Case studies of economies flourishing in peace

Case studies of economies flourishing in peace highlight the profound correlation between stability and prosperity. One notable example is Switzerland, often cited as a model of peace and economic success. With its long-standing neutrality, Switzerland has maintained a stable political environment that fosters innovation and economic growth. The nation's emphasis on education and highly skilled labour has positioned it as a leader in finance, technology, and pharmaceuticals. The Swiss economy benefits from an intricate network of international trade agreements facilitated by its peaceful status, allowing it to thrive as a global hub for business and diplomacy.

Another compelling case is that of post-war Japan. After World War II, Japan embraced a pacifist constitution which, coupled with U.S. support, led to an era of unprecedented economic expansion known as the "Japanese Economic Miracle." This period saw massive investments in technology and infrastructure, coupled with an emphasis on education and workforce development. The peaceful environment allowed for social cohesion and collaboration among companies, which spurred innovation and efficiency. As a result, Japan transformed from a war-torn nation into one of the largest economies in the world, illustrating how peace can catalyse recovery and growth.

Costa Rica offers a unique perspective on peace and economic development. By abolishing its army in 1949, Costa Rica redirected resources toward education, healthcare, and environmental conservation. This focus on human development has led to high literacy rates and a strong emphasis on sustainability, positioning the country as a leader in eco-tourism and renewable energy. The peace dividend has not only improved the quality of life for Costa Ricans but has also attracted foreign investment, further bolstering the economy. The case of Costa Rica exemplifies how prioritizing peace can yield lasting economic benefits while promoting environmental stewardship.

The Nordic countries, including Finland, Sweden, and Norway, present another striking example of the relationship between peace and prosperity. These nations consistently rank high in global peace indices and exhibit robust economies characterised by high levels of social welfare, education, and innovation. Their commitment to social equity and democratic governance has created stable societies where citizens can thrive. This stability fosters an environment conducive to business, leading to high levels of entrepreneurship and economic resilience. The Nordic model demonstrates that peace, coupled with social investment, can create a prosperous economic landscape.

In summary, examining these case studies reveals a clear pattern: peaceful societies tend to flourish economically. The historical examples of Switzerland, Japan, Costa Rica, and the Nordic countries illustrate that peace not only enhances individual well-being but also promotes sustainable economic development. As nations strive for stability, these cases serve as powerful reminders of the priceless value of world peace, reinforcing the notion that fostering peaceful relations is crucial for long-term prosperity and social advancement.

Chapter 20: Mental health and peaceful societies

Mental health is intricately linked to the stability and harmony within societies, underscoring the importance of peaceful environments for individual and collective well-being. In societies marked by conflict and unrest, individuals often experience heightened levels of stress, anxiety, and depression. Conversely, peaceful societies tend to foster environments where mental health can flourish, allowing individuals to develop resilience and emotional well-being. Research has shown that the absence of violence and the presence of social cohesion significantly contribute to lower rates of mental health disorders, illustrating that global peace is not merely a lofty ideal but a crucial component of a healthy population.

The economic benefits of peace extend beyond immediate financial gains; they influence the mental health landscape of communities. Peaceful societies tend to experience greater economic stability, which directly impacts individuals' mental well-being. Stable economies provide access to essential services, including mental health care, education, and social support systems. When individuals feel secure in their economic circumstances, they are less likely to experience anxiety and stress related to survival, thereby promoting a healthier mental state. This interconnection suggests that investing in peace can lead to long-term economic benefits while simultaneously enhancing the mental health of the populace.

Education plays a pivotal role in promoting both peace and mental health. Educational systems that emphasize conflict resolution, empathy, and cultural understanding can significantly reduce the likelihood of violence and discrimination. Moreover, education equips individuals with the tools to engage in constructive dialogues, fostering a culture of peace that contributes to mental well-being. Schools that prioritize mental health education create supportive environments where students learn to manage their emotions and develop healthy relationships, further contributing to a peaceful society where mental health is valued and prioritised.

Personal Stories: Transformations through peace

Across the globe, individuals have experienced profound transformations as a result of peace initiatives in their communities. These personal stories highlight how the cessation of conflict and the establishment of stable environments can lead to remarkable changes in people's lives. For instance, in a war-torn region, a former soldier shared how he transitioned from a life of violence to becoming a community leader advocating for peace. His journey illustrates the potential for personal redemption and the important role that individuals can play in fostering a culture of peace. Such narratives underscore the idea that when peace prevails, individuals can reclaim their lives and contribute positively to society.

A small business owner in a previously conflict-ridden area recounted how peace allowed her to expand her operations and hire more employees. She described how economic opportunities flourished as local markets reopened and international investments returned. This personal experience emphasises the economic benefits of peace, not only for individuals but also for communities as a whole. The ripple effect of economic growth can lead to improved living standards and reduced poverty, further reinforcing the value of maintaining peaceful relations.

A mental health professional working in a post-conflict environment shared stories of clients who experienced a renewed sense of hope and purpose in their lives after peace was established. These individuals reported lower levels of anxiety and depression, as the fear of violence and instability diminished. Their testimonies reveal the deep connection between peace and mental health, highlighting how a peaceful environment fosters resilience and encourages personal growth. The stories of these individuals serve as powerful reminders of the transformative power of peace on psychological well-being.

A farmer living in a conflict-free region described how collaborative efforts in agricultural practices led to more sustainable farming techniques. He noted that with the absence of conflict, communities could focus on environmental stewardship, fostering a culture of cooperation and shared responsibility for natural resources. This transformation not only benefits the environment but also promotes long-term economic stability, as sustainable practices can lead to healthier ecosystems and a more resilient agricultural sector. Such examples illustrate how peace can provide a foundation for environmental initiatives that benefit both current and future generations.

Education plays a crucial role in promoting and sustaining peace, as evidenced by the experiences of students in a post-conflict society. A young woman shared her journey of receiving an education in a newly established peace-oriented school. She spoke of how the curriculum emphasised conflict resolution and cultural understanding, empowering her and her peers to become advocates for peace within their communities. Her story reflects the transformative power of education in shaping future generations who are equipped to foster harmony and cooperation. By investing in education, societies can cultivate a culture of peace, ensuring that the benefits of stability are passed down, leading to lasting transformations across generations. In a rather similar case, I have found myself communicating with fellow former students some of whom I can discuss important issues with confidence that they will understand and think seriously about maintaining the old status quo of "former school-mate friendship" which was nothing less than human happiness. During my university years in USA and in United Kingdom, I had roommates from Korea, Germany, Iran, Iraq, France, Netherlands, Japan, Saudi Arabia, Palestine, Haiti, Australia, Zimbabwe, Egypt, China, Turkey, USSR, Italy and a few more from Asian countries. The truth is, some of these guys have visited me over the years. Therefore, it is true that young people form solid friendship that can help to solve some of the problems that we face today.

Case Studies of successful educational Initiatives

Case studies of successful educational initiatives reveal the profound impact that education can have on promoting world peace and stability. One notable example is the "Peace Education Program" implemented in Colombia, where decades of internal conflict have left deep scars on society. This initiative was designed to foster a culture of peace among youth by integrating conflict resolution, tolerance, and social cohesion into school curricula. Educators trained in peace pedagogy facilitated discussions and activities that encouraged students to engage with differing perspectives and resolve conflicts amicably. The program's success is evident in the reduction of violence in schools and the increased participation of youth in community-building activities.

Another significant case is the Global Citizenship Education (GCE) initiative launched by UNESCO, which aims to equip learners with the knowledge, skills, and values necessary to address global challenges. Through GCE, students are encouraged to think critically about issues such as poverty, inequality, and environmental sustainability. Schools in various countries have reported that students involved in GCE programs demonstrate a heightened sense of responsibility and a commitment to social justice. This initiative illustrates how educational frameworks can cultivate a generation of informed and engaged citizens ready to contribute to global peace efforts.

In Kenya, the "Peace Clubs" established in schools provide another compelling example of how educational initiatives can actively promote peace. These clubs empower students to become advocates for peace in their communities by facilitating dialogue and organising peace-related events. The involvement of students in these clubs has led to a notable decrease in inter-ethnic tensions, particularly during election periods. By fostering leadership skills and encouraging civic engagement, the Peace Clubs have created a ripple effect that extends beyond the school environment, promoting harmony and understanding among diverse groups.

The "Building Bridges" program in South Africa exemplifies the role of education in healing societal divisions. This initiative focuses on reconciliation and social cohesion by bringing together students from historically divided communities to participate in joint educational activities. Through collaborative projects and cultural exchanges, students learn to appreciate each other's backgrounds and work towards common goals. The impact of such initiatives is profound; participants often emerge with a renewed sense of hope and a commitment to fostering inclusive environments, thereby contributing to a more peaceful society.

The importance of global citizenship education

Global citizenship education is essential in fostering a collective understanding of our interconnectedness in a rapidly changing world. It equips individuals with the knowledge, skills, and attitudes necessary to navigate complex global issues, such as conflict, inequality, and environmental degradation. By promoting a sense of belonging to a broader human community, this form of education encourages empathy and respect for diversity. Understanding that local actions can have global consequences empowers individuals to contribute positively to their communities and the world, making global citizenship education a cornerstone of efforts towards world peace.

Chapter 21: Historical case studies of peace and prosperity

The UN and global peace initiatives

The United Nations (UN) has been a pivotal force in promoting global peace initiatives since its establishment in 1945. Created in the aftermath of World War II, the UN aimed to prevent future conflicts through collective security, diplomacy, and international cooperation. Over the decades, the organisation has implemented numerous peacekeeping missions, facilitated negotiations to resolve conflicts, and established various programs aimed at fostering sustainable peace. Through its various agencies and initiatives, the UN has sought to address the root causes of conflict, promote human rights, and encourage economic development, all of which are essential for maintaining global stability.

One of the central tenets of the UN's peace initiatives is the promotion of economic stability as a foundation for lasting peace. The UN recognizes that poverty, inequality, and lack of opportunity are significant drivers of conflict. Programs focusing on economic development, such as the Sustainable Development Goals (SDGs), aim to reduce poverty and create equitable economic opportunities. By addressing these economic disparities, the UN helps to create an environment conducive to peace. The relationship between economic stability and peace is evident in regions where development initiatives have successfully mitigated tensions and fostered cooperation among previously conflicting groups.

Regional success stories

In East Asia, the transformation of post-war Japan into a global economic powerhouse demonstrates the economic benefits of peace. After World War II, Japan embraced a pacifist constitution, prioritising economic development and international cooperation over military expansion. This strategic shift allowed for significant investment in education and technology, culminating in rapid industrial growth and innovation. Japan's success story underscores how peace can create an environment conducive to economic stability, attracting foreign investment and fostering entrepreneurial endeavours, ultimately leading to a prosperous society.

In the case of Rwanda, which has made remarkable strides in healing and recovery since the 1994 genocide. The country has prioritized reconciliation and community engagement, leading to significant improvements in mental health and societal trust. Initiatives such as the "Gacaca" courts allowed for community-based justice and dialogue, enabling individuals to confront their trauma collectively. This emphasis on healing in a peaceful context has had profound implications for the well-being of Rwandans, showcasing how peace can facilitate psychological recovery and foster a supportive community environment.

In South Africa following the end of apartheid, the establishment of integrated schools and peace education programs has been pivotal in fostering understanding and cooperation among diverse communities. These educational efforts have empowered the youth to engage actively in peacebuilding processes, highlighting the crucial role that education plays in nurturing a culture of peace. By investing in educational initiatives that promote dialogue and mutual respect, societies can cultivate future generations committed to maintaining peace and stability, ensuring long-term prosperity.

Historical peace processes provide invaluable lessons that can guide contemporary efforts toward achieving and sustaining global peace. One of the fundamental insights drawn from these processes is the importance of inclusivity in negotiations. Successful peace agreements often arise from the active participation of diverse stakeholders, including marginalised groups, women, and youth. By ensuring that all voices are heard, peace processes not only gain legitimacy but also address the root causes of conflict, leading to more durable and comprehensive solutions. For instance, the peace accords in Colombia highlighted the necessity of including various social sectors, which ultimately contributed to a more stable post-conflict society.

Another critical lesson is the role of trust-building measures in facilitating dialogue and negotiation. Historical peace processes, such as the Good Friday Agreement in Northern Ireland, demonstrate that establishing trust between conflicting parties is essential for moving forward. Confidence-building measures, such as ceasefires and the demilitarisation of certain areas, play a pivotal role in creating a conducive environment for dialogue. These measures help to alleviate fears and suspicions, allowing negotiators to focus on substantive issues rather than being mired in past grievances. The experience from these processes underscores the need for patience and gradual progress in peacebuilding efforts.

Furthermore, historical peace processes reveal the significance of addressing economic disparities and the socio-economic dimensions of conflict. Economic stability is often a precursor to lasting peace; thus, peace agreements that incorporate economic recovery plans tend to yield better results. The post-war reconstruction efforts in Germany after World War II, exemplified by the Marshall Plan, illustrate how economic investment can facilitate not only recovery but also the establishment of enduring peace. Addressing economic inequalities and fostering development can prevent the resurgence of conflict by creating a sense of shared prosperity among different community groups.

Chapter 22: The role of international organisations

The role of international organisations in fostering world peace is integral to maintaining global stability and addressing the multifaceted challenges that threaten it. Organisations such as the United Nations (UN), the World Health Organisation (WHO), and the World Trade Organisation (WTO) play pivotal roles in mediating conflicts, promoting cooperation, and offering platforms for dialogue among nations. By providing frameworks for international laws and norms, these organisations facilitate diplomatic relations and help nations navigate disputes without resorting to violence. Their efforts not only contribute to immediate conflict resolution but also lay the groundwork for long-term peacebuilding and stability.

International organisations also contribute significantly to the economic benefits of global stability and peace. By fostering trade agreements, promoting economic cooperation, and providing financial assistance for development projects, they help create environments conducive to economic growth. A peaceful world enables countries to allocate resources toward development rather than military expenditures. This shift allows for investments in education, healthcare, and infrastructure, ultimately improving quality of life and enhancing global prosperity. Regions that enjoy the support of international organisations often experience reduced poverty and increased opportunities, underscoring the link between peace and economic development.

Case studies of successful collaborations

One prominent case is the European Union, which emerged after World War II as a response to the devastating conflicts that plagued the continent. Initially focused on economic cooperation, the EU has evolved into a multifaceted union that promotes political stability, economic prosperity, and cultural exchange among its member states. This collaboration has not only contributed to a remarkable period of peace in Europe but has also served as a model for other regions seeking to overcome historical animosities through shared goals and mutual benefits.

Another significant example is the peacebuilding efforts in Colombia, where decades of conflict had resulted in profound social and economic disruption. The 2016 peace agreement between the Colombian government and the Revolutionary Armed Forces of Colombia (FARC) marked a turning point in the nation's history. This collaboration involved extensive dialogue, compromise, and the participation of various stakeholders, including civil society and international organisations. The agreement facilitated a transformative process aimed at addressing root causes of violence while promoting social justice and inclusion, ultimately demonstrating how collaborative peace efforts can yield long-lasting benefits for individuals and communities.

In the realm of environmental sustainability, the collaborative efforts of countries in the Arctic region highlight how shared interests can foster peace. The Arctic Council, comprising eight Arctic nations, has facilitated cooperation on environmental protection, sustainable development, and scientific research in this sensitive region. By prioritizing shared ecological concerns over territorial disputes, these nations have been able to maintain a peaceful coexistence, underscoring the notion that collaboration on environmental issues can serve as a foundation for broader peace initiatives. This case illustrates how environmental sustainability can intertwine with peacebuilding, reinforcing the idea that addressing global challenges together can mitigate conflict potential.

Strategies for Effective Global Partnerships

Building effective global partnerships is essential for promoting world peace and stability. One of the primary strategies is fostering open communication among nations, organisations, and communities. Transparent dialogue can bridge cultural and ideological divides, creating an environment conducive to understanding and collaboration. By establishing regular forums for discussion, stakeholders can share their perspectives, concerns, and aspirations, which is vital in resolving conflicts and preventing misunderstandings.

Chapter 23: Health in conflict vs. peaceful societies

Health in conflict-affected regions is often undermined by the chaos and instability that accompany warfare, leading to significant morbidity and mortality. Conflict disrupts healthcare systems, making it difficult for individuals to access essential medical services. Hospitals may be damaged or destroyed, healthcare personnel may flee, and medical supplies can become scarce. In such environments, preventable diseases can resurge, maternal and child health can decline, and mental health issues can exacerbate, resulting in a public health crisis. The psychological toll of living in conflict zones, including trauma, anxiety, and depression, further complicates health outcomes and reduces overall life expectancy.

In contrast, peaceful societies tend to enjoy better health indicators. Access to healthcare is typically more reliable in stable environments, allowing for effective disease prevention, management of chronic conditions, and timely medical intervention. Countries characterized by peace often invest in public health initiatives, promoting healthy lifestyles and preventive care. For instance, vaccination programs and health education campaigns can thrive in peaceful settings, leading to lower incidence rates of infectious diseases and improved maternal and child health metrics. The correlation between peace and better health outcomes underscores the fundamental importance of stability for the well-being of populations.

Moreover, violence disrupts the social fabric of communities, leading to diminished trust and cohesion among residents. This fragmentation can result in reduced access to essential healthcare services, as individuals may feel unsafe seeking care or may avoid clinics due to fear of violence. Additionally, the economic implications of violence can lead to increased healthcare costs, as injuries and associated health conditions require ongoing treatment. This strain on public health resources can divert attention and funding away from preventive measures and other vital health initiatives, exacerbating existing health disparities.

The relationship between violence and health outcomes is particularly pronounced in vulnerable populations, including children and the elderly. For children, exposure to violence can hinder cognitive development and lead to behavioural issues, which can perpetuate cycles of violence and health deterioration across generations. The elderly, on the other hand, may face exacerbated health risks due to the stress and trauma associated with violent environments. Both groups require targeted interventions to mitigate these effects and promote resilience, underscoring the urgent need for comprehensive public health strategies that consider the broader implications of violence.

Ultimately, the link between peace and health outcomes highlights the importance of global cooperation in addressing the root causes of violence. Collaborative efforts among nations, supported by educational initiatives and technological advancements, can facilitate dialogue and understanding, paving the way for sustainable peace. By recognising the intrinsic value of peace as a catalyst for improved public health, societies can work together to build a healthier and more resilient world, benefiting current and future generations alike.

Chapter 24: Successful youth-led peace movements

Successful youth-led peace movements have emerged as powerful catalysts for change, demonstrating the remarkable capabilities of young people to advocate for peace and social justice. These movements harness the energy, creativity, and idealism of youth, often leading to significant shifts in societal attitudes towards conflict resolution and reconciliation. The role of youth in peacebuilding is not merely supplementary; it is essential, as their innovative approaches and grassroots mobilisation can influence national and international dialogues on peace.

One prominent example of a successful youth-led peace movement is the "Youth for Peace" initiative in Colombia, which has mobilised thousands of young people to engage in dialogues aimed at resolving long-standing conflicts. By using artistic expression, social media campaigns, and community engagement, these young activists have drawn attention to the impact of violence on their lives and have proposed constructive alternatives to conflict. Their efforts have not only raised awareness but have also led to policy changes and increased participation of youth in peace processes, demonstrating how young voices can shape the future.

In the Middle East, the "Seeds of Peace" program has brought together youth from conflicting backgrounds, fostering relationships and understanding through dialogue and education. This initiative focuses on empowering young leaders with conflict resolution skills, encouraging them to act as agents of change in their communities. By facilitating cross-cultural exchanges and promoting collaborative projects, the program has cultivated a generation of peace advocates who are committed to breaking the cycles of violence and fostering a culture of coexistence.

The economic benefits of youth-led peace movements are significant. When young people actively participate in peacebuilding efforts, they contribute to the establishment of stable societies, which in turn attract investment, create jobs, and foster sustainable development. Countries that engage their youth in peace initiatives often experience improved social cohesion and economic resilience, leading to a virtuous cycle of prosperity and stability. This underscores the notion that investing in youth-led movements not only promotes peace but also enhances economic opportunities for entire communities.

Moreover, the psychological impacts of engaging youth in peace movements are profound. Participation in peace efforts can instil a sense of purpose and belonging among young people, promoting mental well-being and resilience. In environments plagued by violence and instability, offering youth a platform to express their hopes and aspirations cultivates a sense of agency and empowerment. As these young peacebuilders witness the tangible results of their efforts, they develop a strong commitment to ongoing peace initiatives, reinforcing the idea that their contributions are invaluable to the collective pursuit of a more peaceful world.

Strategies for enhancing youth participation

Strategies for enhancing youth participation in peace initiatives involve a multifaceted approach that recognises the unique perspectives and potential of young people. Engaging youth in discussions about peace not only empowers them but also fosters a sense of responsibility towards global stability. One effective strategy is to create platforms for youth dialogue, where they can express their views, share experiences, and propose solutions to local and global challenges. These platforms can take the form of community forums, online discussions, or youth-led conferences that encourage collaboration and idea-sharing among diverse groups.

Another essential strategy is the integration of peace education into existing curricula. By introducing concepts of conflict resolution, empathy, and global citizenship early in educational settings, young people can develop the skills necessary to navigate and contribute to peaceful societies. Schools and educational institutions should partner with organisations focused on peacebuilding to provide interactive workshops and training sessions that equip students with practical tools for advocacy and activism. This proactive approach can inspire students to take initiative in their communities, promoting a culture of peace from a young age.

Mentorship programs can also play a pivotal role in enhancing youth engagement. Connecting young individuals with experienced peacebuilders, community leaders, and activists can provide invaluable guidance and support. Mentorship creates opportunities for youth to learn from the successes and challenges faced by others, encouraging them to develop their own projects and initiatives. By fostering relationships between generations, these programs can bridge knowledge gaps and create a supportive network that amplifies youth voices in peace initiatives.

Utilizing technology and social media is a powerful strategy for reaching and mobilizing young people. Digital platforms allow for the rapid dissemination of information and can be leveraged to spread awareness about peace initiatives globally. Social media campaigns can engage youth in meaningful conversations, encouraging them to take action and participate in peacebuilding efforts. Additionally, online tools can facilitate collaboration among young peace advocates across borders, enabling them to share resources, strategies, and success stories that inspire collective action.

Finally, recognising and celebrating youth contributions to peace initiatives is crucial for sustaining their engagement. Public acknowledgment through awards, recognitions, and showcases of successful projects can motivate young individuals and inspire their peers. Highlighting stories of youth-led initiatives that have made a positive impact on communities can reinforce the idea that young people are vital agents of change. By fostering an environment that values and uplifts youth participation, societies can cultivate a generation committed to promoting peace and stability on a global scale.

Chapter 25: Digital platforms for peace-building

Digital platforms have emerged as powerful tools in the realm of peacebuilding, providing innovative avenues for dialogue, collaboration, and the sharing of resources among diverse stakeholders. These platforms allow individuals, organisations, and governments to connect in ways that were previously unimaginable, breaking down geographical barriers and fostering a sense of global community. With the rapid advancement of technology, digital platforms can facilitate peace initiatives that not only address immediate conflicts but also promote long-term stability and understanding among different cultures and nations. The integration of technology in peacebuilding efforts has the potential to transform how societies engage with one another, making peace more accessible and actionable.

One of the significant advantages of digital platforms is their ability to amplify marginalized voices in peacebuilding discussions. Historically, many peace processes have excluded certain groups, particularly those from underrepresented communities. Social media, online forums, and other digital communication tools empower these voices, enabling them to share their experiences and perspectives on conflict and peace. This inclusivity can lead to more comprehensive and representative peace agreements, as it ensures that the needs and concerns of all affected parties are considered. By leveraging technology, peacebuilders can create spaces for dialogue that honour diversity and foster mutual understanding.

Moreover, digital platforms facilitate education and awareness around peacebuilding, allowing for the dissemination of important information and resources on a global scale. Online courses, webinars, and interactive content can educate individuals about the principles of peace and conflict resolution, equipping them with the skills necessary to engage in peacebuilding initiatives.

This educational approach can have far-reaching impacts, as it enhances the capacity of individuals and communities to contribute to peaceful societies. Furthermore, the accessibility of information via digital platforms can inspire youth engagement in peace initiatives, encouraging a new generation to take an active role in advocating for global stability and harmony.

International cooperation is another crucial area where digital platforms play a pivotal role in peacebuilding efforts. These platforms enable collaboration among governments, non-governmental organisations, and civil society groups across borders. By facilitating partnerships and networks, digital tools can enhance the effectiveness of peace initiatives, allowing for the pooling of resources, knowledge, and experiences. Such collaboration is essential in addressing complex global challenges that require coordinated responses, from humanitarian crises to environmental sustainability. Through international cooperation facilitated by technology, the global community can work together more effectively to promote peace and stability.

In addition to fostering dialogue and collaboration, digital platforms have the potential to support mental health and well-being in conflict-affected areas. Access to information on health resources, psychological support, and community-building initiatives can improve individual well-being in societies recovering from violence. By promoting mental health awareness and providing tools for resilience, these platforms can help individuals and communities heal and thrive. Ultimately, the integration of digital technology into peacebuilding efforts is not only about conflict resolution but also about nurturing the holistic well-being of people, contributing to a more peaceful and prosperous world for all.

Innovations in communication have emerged as pivotal tools for conflict resolution, reshaping the landscape of how individuals and nations engage in dialogue. Traditional methods of communication often fell short in addressing the complexities of modern conflicts, leading to misunderstandings and prolonged tensions.

Another innovative approach is the use of artificial intelligence and data analytics in conflict resolution. AI can analyse vast amounts of data from various sources to identify patterns and predict potential flashpoints before they escalate into violence. This proactive approach allows for timely interventions and the crafting of tailored communication strategies aimed at addressing the root causes of conflict. Additionally, AI-driven platforms can help facilitate negotiations by suggesting compromises based on historical outcomes, thereby enhancing the likelihood of successful resolutions.

The future of technology and peace initiatives

The future of technology is poised to play a transformative role in peace initiatives across the globe. As digital connectivity expands, the potential for technology to foster dialogue and understanding among diverse cultures and nations increases. Innovations such as social media platforms, virtual reality, and artificial intelligence create avenues for storytelling and collaboration that were previously unimaginable. These tools can bridge gaps in communication, allowing for the sharing of experiences and perspectives that can lead to greater empathy and cooperation among individuals from different backgrounds.

Moreover, technology facilitates the monitoring and implementation of peace agreements. Advanced data analytics and satellite imagery can help track compliance with ceasefires and peace treaties, ensuring that all parties adhere to their commitments. Tools like blockchain technology can provide transparency and security in financial transactions related to humanitarian aid, reducing the likelihood of corruption and misallocation of resources. By leveraging technology for accountability and transparency, organisations can help build trust among conflicting parties, which is essential for lasting peace.

In addition to fostering dialogue and monitoring compliance, technology can also enhance economic stability in regions affected by conflict. E-commerce platforms can empower local businesses by providing access to broader markets, while mobile banking services can improve financial inclusion for underserved populations. These economic opportunities help to mitigate the conditions that often lead to conflict, as individuals and communities experience improved livelihoods and greater social cohesion. By investing in technological solutions that promote economic development, peace initiatives can create a foundation for sustainable stability.

The psychological impacts of peace on individual well-being are also increasingly recognized within the context of technology. Mental health apps and online support networks can provide individuals affected by conflict with crucial resources for healing and recovery. Moreover, educational technologies that promote peacebuilding curricula can empower youth with the knowledge and skills needed to foster a culture of peace. By addressing the psychological needs of individuals and communities, technology can contribute to a more resilient society, better equipped to handle conflicts without resorting to violence.

Chapter 26: Illegal occupation and international law

Definition of occupation

Occupation, in the context of international law, refers to the control and governance of a territory by a foreign military force without the consent of the sovereign authority. This situation often arises during armed conflict, where one state invades another and asserts its dominance over the occupied territory. The legal framework governing occupation is primarily derived from the Hague Conventions of 1899 and 1907, along with the Fourth Geneva Convention of 1949. These documents outline the rights and obligations of occupying powers, emphasising the protection of civilian populations and the preservation of public order and civil life.

According to international law, an occupation is considered illegal if it is established through aggressive warfare or if it fails to meet the established legal criteria. The principle of self-determination, enshrined in the United Nations Charter, asserts that peoples have the right to determine their political status and pursue their economic, social, and cultural development. Consequently, any attempt by a state to occupy another territory against the will of its people is viewed as a violation of both international law and human rights. This legal framework seeks to prevent the expansion of territorial control through military means and to uphold the sovereignty of nations.

The responsibilities of an occupying power are explicitly outlined in international law. These include ensuring the safety and well-being of the civilian population, maintaining public order, and respecting the local laws of the occupied territory. Importantly, the occupying force is prohibited from altering the demographic makeup of the area, exploiting its resources for its own benefit, or undertaking actions that may lead to violations of human rights. Such actions can lead to severe consequences for both the occupying power and the occupied population, including international condemnation and potential legal repercussions.

Human rights violations during occupation are a significant concern. Civilians often endure hardships such as forced displacement, unlawful killings, arbitrary detention, and restrictions on their freedom of movement. The occupying power's failure to adhere to international legal standards can lead to widespread suffering and long-lasting trauma for the affected populations. Moreover, these violations can exacerbate tensions and contribute to ongoing conflict, undermining efforts for peace and reconciliation in the region.

In summary, the definition of occupation extends beyond mere territorial control; it encompasses the legal and ethical obligations that an occupying power must uphold. The principles established by international law serve to safeguard human rights and the dignity of individuals living under occupation. It is crucial for the international community to recognise and address violations of these principles to promote justice, accountability, and ultimately, the restoration of peace in affected regions. Understanding the intricacies of occupation not only highlights the importance of legal frameworks but also underscores the necessity of protecting human rights in times of conflict.

Historical context of occupation

The historical context of occupation is crucial for understanding the legal and moral frameworks that govern the conduct of states during times of conflict. Occupation, in the context of international law, typically refers to the control and governance of a territory by a foreign military force. This phenomenon has been prevalent throughout history, often resulting in significant human rights violations and the disregard for the sovereignty of nations. The evolution of legal standards regarding occupation reflects a growing recognition of the need to protect the rights of individuals and communities under foreign control.

The principles governing occupation are primarily derived from the Hague Conventions of 1899 and 1907, which established rules for the conduct of war and the treatment of occupied territories. These conventions introduced the concept of "military occupation," where the occupying power must respect the laws in force in the occupied territory and ensure the welfare of the civilian population. However, the enforcement of these principles has often been inconsistent, leading to widespread abuses. Historical examples, such as the

German occupation of France during World War II or the Israeli occupation of Palestinian territories, illustrate the challenges faced in implementing international legal standards in real-world situations.

In addition to the Hague Conventions, the Fourth Geneva Convention of 1949 further elaborated on the rights of individuals under occupation, emphasising the protection of civilian populations. This framework was developed in response to the atrocities committed during World War II, where millions suffered under foreign rule. The Convention prohibits collective punishments, the transfer of the occupying power's civilian population into the occupied territory, and mandates the humane treatment of all persons. Despite these protections, violations remain prevalent, often justified by the occupying powers under claims of security or national interest.

The historical context also reveals how colonialism has shaped contemporary understandings of occupation. Many modern states emerged from colonial rule, where foreign powers imposed their authority over indigenous populations. This legacy continues to influence international relations and the perception of legitimacy surrounding occupations. As former colonies assert their sovereignty, the international community grapples with the implications of historical injustices that inform current conflicts. The narrative of occupation is thus intertwined with issues of self-determination and the right of peoples to govern themselves free from external domination.

The international community has made significant strides in addressing the legal aspects of occupation, yet challenges persist in holding states accountable for violations. The United Nations and various human rights organisations play critical roles in monitoring and documenting abuses, advocating for the enforcement of international law. However, political considerations often hinder decisive action, allowing violations to continue unchecked. Understanding the historical context of occupation is essential to grasp the complexities of current international law, human rights, and the ongoing struggle for justice and accountability in occupied territories.

Overview of international law

International law serves as a framework for the conduct of states in their interactions with one another, establishing guidelines that govern issues such as war, trade, and human rights. At its core, international law seeks to promote peace and cooperation among nations while protecting fundamental rights and freedoms. The principles of sovereignty and territorial integrity are central to international law, asserting that nations have the right to govern themselves without external interference. This legal structure is particularly crucial in the context of military occupation, where one state exerts control over another without the latter's consent.

The prohibition of forceful occupation is enshrined in various international legal instruments, including the United Nations Charter, which emphasises the inadmissibility of acquiring territory by force. The Charter's Article 2(4) explicitly prohibits the threat or use of force against the territorial integrity or political independence of any state. This foundational principle underlines the notion that occupation without consent is a violation of international law, triggering potential accountability for the occupying power. Furthermore, the Geneva Conventions provide specific protections for civilian populations in occupied territories, aiming to mitigate human suffering and uphold human dignity during conflicts.

In conclusion, understanding the overview of international law is essential for comprehending the complexities surrounding military occupation and human rights. The legal prohibitions against forceful occupation, coupled with the protections afforded to individuals under international law, create a framework designed to promote justice and accountability. As the global landscape continues to evolve, the principles of international law remain a vital tool for addressing injustices and safeguarding human rights in situations of occupation, emphasising the need for continued vigilance and advocacy.

⚬⚬⚬

CUSTOMARY INTERNATIONAL law

Customary international law refers to the unwritten rules that arise from the consistent practice of states, accompanied by a belief that such practices are legally obligatory. This body of law plays a crucial role in regulating state behaviour, particularly in contexts of occupation and conflict. Occupation, defined as the effective control of a territory by foreign armed forces, raises significant legal questions under customary international law. The principles governing occupation aim to protect the rights of the occupied population and limit the powers of the occupying force, ensuring that international law is upheld even in times of conflict.

One of the fundamental tenets of customary international law concerning occupation is that it is illegal for a country to forcefully occupy another sovereign nation. This principle is rooted in the notion of state sovereignty and the right to self-determination. The prohibition against the use of force is enshrined in the United Nations Charter and has been reinforced through various international treaties and declarations. States are not permitted to acquire territory by military conquest, and any attempt to impose control over another nation through force is considered a violation of international law.

Chapter 27: Case studies of occupation

The Israeli-Palestinian conflict

The Israeli-Palestinian conflict is a protracted and complex struggle that has persisted for over a century, emerging from historical, political, and territorial disputes. At its core, the conflict centres on the competing national aspirations of the Jewish and Palestinian peoples. The establishment of the State of Israel in 1948, following the end of the British Mandate in Palestine, marked a significant turning point that led to widespread displacement of Palestinians, known as the Nakba, or "catastrophe." This event laid the groundwork for ongoing tensions, violence, and deep-seated grievances that continue to fuel the conflict today.

International law plays a critical role in understanding the dynamics of the Israeli-Palestinian conflict, particularly the principles regarding occupation. According to the Fourth Geneva Convention, a country is prohibited from acquiring territory by force and from occupying another state's territory unlawfully. The international community overwhelmingly views Israel's occupation of the West Bank and Gaza Strip, which began in 1967, as a violation of these principles. The legal status of these territories remains a contentious issue, with various United Nations resolutions and statements reaffirming the inalienable rights of the Palestinian people to self-determination and sovereignty.

Human rights violations during occupation are a crucial aspect of the Israeli-Palestinian conflict. Reports from numerous human rights organisations have documented instances of excessive use of force, arbitrary detentions, restrictions on movement, and the demolition of homes as tactics employed by Israeli authorities. These actions not only contravene international human rights law but also exacerbate the humanitarian crisis faced by Palestinians living under occupation. The blockade of Gaza, imposed since 2007, has further deteriorated living conditions, leading to widespread poverty, lack of access to basic services, and a profound sense of helplessness among the population.

The impact of occupation extends beyond immediate human rights violations; it also undermines the prospects for a lasting peace. The settlement expansion in the West Bank, deemed illegal under international law, further complicates the peace process by altering the demographic and geographic realities on the ground. This expansion fosters resentment and distrust, making negotiations increasingly difficult. The cycle of violence and retaliation perpetuates a state of insecurity for both Israelis and Palestinians, creating an environment where dialogue and reconciliation seem distant.

In conclusion, the Israeli-Palestinian conflict remains a poignant example of the challenges posed by occupation and the violations of international law. The principles enshrined in international humanitarian law and human rights law are vital for addressing the injustices experienced by the Palestinian people. Acknowledging and upholding these principles is essential for fostering a sustainable resolution to the conflict that respects the rights and aspirations of both Israelis and Palestinians. Only through a commitment to justice, accountability, and dialogue can a path toward peace be forged, ensuring that the lessons of history are not repeated, paradoxically, this has now happened.

The Occupation of Iraq

The occupation of Iraq, following the United States-led invasion in 2003, has been a complex and contentious issue in international law and human rights discourse. The invasion, which was justified by the U.S. government on the grounds of eliminating weapons of mass destruction and toppling Saddam Hussein's regime, has been widely criticised as a violation of international law. According to the United Nations Charter, the use of force against another state is prohibited unless in self-defence or with the authorisation of the Security Council. The absence of a legitimate basis for the invasion raises significant questions about the legality of the subsequent occupation.

International law, particularly the Fourth Geneva Convention, outlines the responsibilities of occupying powers and the rights of the occupied population. These laws are designed to protect civilians and maintain order during occupations. The U.S. occupation of Iraq was marked by a lack of adherence to these legal frameworks, resulting in widespread human rights violations.

Reports from various human rights organisations documented instances of torture, unlawful killings, and the destruction of property, which directly contravened the obligations of an occupying power under international law.

The human rights violations that occurred during the occupation were not isolated incidents but rather systemic issues that reflected a broader disregard for the rights of the Iraqi people. The treatment of detainees at Abu Ghraib prison became emblematic of the failure to uphold human rights standards during the occupation. Graphic images of abuse shocked the world and prompted outrage, highlighting the need for accountability and reform in how occupying forces conduct themselves. The implications of these violations extend beyond the immediate context, as they have contributed to lasting instability and resentment in the region.

Furthermore, the occupation had profound socio-political consequences for Iraq. The dismantling of the Iraqi state apparatus and the disbandment of the army led to a power vacuum and heightened sectarian tensions. The resulting chaos and violence were exacerbated by the failure to implement a cohesive strategy for rebuilding the nation. This lack of planning and respect for Iraqi sovereignty not only undermined the initial objectives of the invasion but also raised ethical questions about the responsibility of the occupying power to facilitate a stable and just transition for the occupied populace.

In the aftermath of the occupation, the legal and moral implications of the invasion continue to resonate in discussions of international law and human rights. The case of Iraq serves as a cautionary tale about the consequences of military intervention without adequate justification or regard for the rule of law. As the international community reflects on the lessons learned from this occupation, it becomes increasingly clear that the principles of sovereignty, self-determination, and human rights must remain central to any discourse on military intervention and occupation in the future.

Western Sahara

Western Sahara, a territory located in North Africa, has been the subject of a protracted conflict characterised by issues of occupation, self-determination, and human rights violations. The territory was a Spanish colony until 1975, when Spain withdrew, leading to a power vacuum that resulted in a territorial dispute between Morocco and the Sahrawi Arab Democratic Republic (SADR), which is proclaimed by the Polisario Front. The international community has largely recognised Western Sahara as a non-self-governing territory, yet Morocco's ongoing control over the region raises significant questions regarding international law and the rights of its indigenous population.

Under international law, particularly the principles outlined in the United Nations Charter and the Declaration on the Granting of Independence to Colonial Countries and Peoples, the right to self-determination is paramount. The Sahrawi people, who are the native inhabitants of Western Sahara, have repeatedly expressed their desire for independence and self-governance. However, Morocco's military presence and administrative practices in the region have created a situation of de facto occupation, which is widely viewed as illegal under international law. The continued assertion of Moroccan sovereignty over the territory complicates the prospects for a peaceful resolution and undermines the rights of the Sahrawi people.

Human rights violations have been reported extensively in Western Sahara, particularly against those who advocate for Sahrawi independence. Reports from various human rights organisations indicate that individuals advocating for self-determination face harassment, arbitrary detention, and even torture. The Moroccan authorities have implemented strict controls over freedom of expression, assembly, and association, severely limiting the ability of Sahrawis to voice their opinions or organise peacefully. Such actions not only contravene international human rights standards but also raise profound ethical concerns regarding the treatment of populations under occupation.

Efforts to resolve the situation in Western Sahara have included various diplomatic initiatives led by the United Nations, aimed at facilitating a referendum on self-determination for the Sahrawi people. However, progress has been stymied by disagreements between Morocco and the Polisario Front, often exacerbated by geopolitical interests in the region. The lack of a resolution has allowed human rights abuses to persist, as the international community struggles to uphold its commitments to protect the rights of individuals living under foreign occupation. This ongoing failure highlights the need for a renewed commitment to international law and the principles of human rights in addressing the plight of the Sahrawi people.

The situation in Western Sahara serves as a poignant reminder of the complexities surrounding occupation, sovereignty, and human rights. It underscores the importance of international legal frameworks designed to protect vulnerable populations from the consequences of foreign domination. As the world grapples with the implications of occupation and the responsibilities of states under international law, the case of Western Sahara stands as a critical touchstone for understanding the broader challenges associated with rights, justice, and self-determination in occupied territories.

Chapter 28: Violations of human rights during occupation

Types of human rights violations

Human rights violations can take many forms, particularly in the context of military occupation. When one country forcefully occupies another, it often leads to a range of abuses that undermine the dignity and rights of individuals living in the occupied territory. These violations can include physical violence, such as torture and extrajudicial killings, as well as psychological abuses that instil fear and trauma within the population. The systematic nature of these violations often reflects a broader strategy of repression aimed at controlling the local populace and suppressing dissent.

One significant type of violation is the denial of the right to life, which can occur through direct actions such as killings, as well as through indirect means, such as restricting access to essential services like healthcare and clean water. During occupations, military forces may engage in lethal actions against civilians, justifying these acts under the guise of security measures. This not only results in immediate loss of life but also creates an environment of fear and instability, further compromising the safety and well-being of the populace.

Another prevalent violation is the infringement of personal freedoms and liberties. Occupied individuals often face restrictions on their freedom of movement, which can be enforced through checkpoints, curfews, and even outright bans on travel. Such restrictions are designed to limit the ability of the local population to organise, protest, or seek international assistance. Additionally, freedom of expression is frequently curtailed, with media censorship and suppression of dissenting voices becoming commonplace. These actions serve to stifle any opposition to the occupying forces and consolidate their control over the territory.

Economic rights also suffer during occupations, as the occupying power may exploit local resources for its own benefit, leading to widespread poverty and deprivation. This exploitation can manifest in various ways, including the appropriation of land, destruction of businesses, and manipulation of local economies to serve the needs of the occupiers. Such actions not only violate the right to an adequate standard of living but also contribute to long-term socio-economic instability, making recovery and rebuilding efforts increasingly difficult for the affected community.

Finally, cultural rights are often under threat in occupied territories. The imposition of the occupying power's culture and values can lead to the erosion of local traditions and identities. This may involve the destruction of cultural heritage sites, restrictions on religious practices, and efforts to alter the educational system to align with the occupier's ideology. Such violations not only harm the immediate cultural landscape but also threaten the very fabric of the community, as cultural identity plays a critical role in the resilience and unity of people facing oppression. Understanding these various types of violations is essential for recognising the broader implications of military occupation on human rights and the need for accountability and justice.

Documented cases of abuse

Documented cases of abuse during military occupations highlight the stark violations of international law and the fundamental rights of affected populations. Historical and contemporary instances illustrate how occupying forces often disregard the legal frameworks established to protect civilians. The Geneva Conventions, particularly, set forth the obligations of occupying powers to ensure the well-being of the occupied populace, yet violations are frequently reported, raising serious concerns about accountability and justice.

One notable case is the Israeli occupation of Palestinian territories, which has been marked by extensive reports of human rights abuses. Various organisations, including Human Rights Watch and Amnesty International, have documented incidents of unlawful killings, forced evictions, and the demolition of homes. The Israeli military's policies and practices in these territories have been criticised for violating the Fourth Geneva Convention, which prohibits collective punishment and mandates the protection of civilian property. These documented abuses serve as a reminder of the dire consequences faced by civilians under prolonged military occupation.

In more recent times, the occupation of Crimea by Russia has raised significant human rights concerns. Reports of arbitrary detentions, enforced disappearances, and the suppression of political dissent have emerged since the annexation in 2014. The United Nations and various human rights organisations have condemned these actions as violations of international law, emphasising the need for accountability for those perpetrating such abuses. The situation in Crimea underscores the ongoing relevance of international legal frameworks in addressing the rights of individuals in occupied territories.

These documented cases of abuse during occupations underscore the critical importance of adhering to international law and human rights standards. They reveal a pattern of neglect and violation that must be addressed to ensure the protection of civilians. The international community has a responsibility to hold accountable those who commit such abuses and to advocate for the rights of individuals living under occupation. Understanding these cases is essential in the broader discourse on the legality of military occupations and the imperative of upholding human rights in the face of conflict.

The United Nations (UN) plays a pivotal role in addressing issues related to occupation through its various agencies and frameworks. Established in the aftermath of World War II, the UN was created to promote international cooperation and maintain peace. One of its primary functions is to uphold international law, particularly in situations of armed conflict and occupation. The UN's Charter, along with numerous resolutions and treaties, provides a legal framework that guides the conduct of nations in times of war and occupation, highlighting the principle that forceful occupation is illegal under international law.

Chapter 29: International Court of Justice

The International Court of Justice (ICJ), established in 1945 as the principal judicial organ of the United Nations, plays a pivotal role in the realm of international law, particularly in addressing issues of state sovereignty and occupation. The ICJ is tasked with resolving disputes between states and providing advisory opinions on legal questions referred to it by UN organs and specialised agencies. Its jurisdiction encompasses a wide range of matters, including those related to the legality of the use of force, territorial disputes, and violations of international human rights law. The court's decisions are binding on the parties involved, though it has no direct means of enforcing its rulings, relying instead on the compliance of states.

The cornerstone of the ICJ's work is the principle that it is illegal for a country to forcefully occupy another country. This principle is embedded in various international treaties and customary international law, including the UN Charter and the Geneva Conventions. The court has affirmed this stance in several landmark cases, emphasising that occupation must be conducted in accordance with international law, particularly with respect to the rights and welfare of the occupied population. Violations of these obligations can lead to significant legal repercussions and contribute to the broader discourse on human rights and humanitarian law.

One of the notable cases that illustrates the ICJ's role in adjudicating issues of occupation is the advisory opinion regarding the legality of the construction of a wall in the Occupied Palestinian Territory. In this 2004 opinion, the ICJ concluded that the wall's construction violated international law and that Israel, as the occupying power, had obligations toward the Palestinian population. This ruling underscored the court's commitment to upholding human rights standards during situations of occupation and provided a legal framework for understanding the implications of such actions on the rights of individuals living under occupation.

Furthermore, the ICJ's decisions contribute to the development of international law by clarifying the obligations of occupying powers. The court has highlighted that not only must the occupiers refrain from infringing upon the rights of the occupied, but they must also take affirmative steps to ensure the well-being and protection of the civilian population. This includes providing access to essential services, respecting cultural identities, and facilitating humanitarian assistance. As such, the ICJ not only addresses individual cases but also shapes the broader legal landscape regarding occupation rights and human rights protections.

In conclusion, the International Court of Justice serves as a crucial institution in the enforcement and interpretation of international law concerning occupation and human rights. Its rulings provide important legal precedents that guide state behaviour and promote accountability. As global conflicts continue to arise, the ICJ remains a vital forum for ensuring that the principles of law and human rights are upheld, reinforcing the message that occupation, when unjustified, is not only a violation of sovereignty but also a breach of fundamental human rights norms. Through its work, the ICJ seeks to foster peace and justice in an increasingly complex international environment.

Chapter 30: Paths to justice and accountability

Mechanisms for addressing violations

Mechanisms for addressing violations of international law and human rights during instances of occupation are critical to ensuring accountability and justice. Various international legal frameworks and institutions exist to respond to breaches of these norms. The United Nations (UN) plays a pivotal role in this context, with its various bodies established to monitor, report, and act upon violations. The UN Security Council, for instance, can impose sanctions or authorise peacekeeping missions in response to aggressive occupations that violate international law. Additionally, the UN Human Rights Council conducts investigations into alleged human rights violations, providing a platform for victims and fostering international awareness.

International courts and tribunals also serve as essential mechanisms for addressing violations. The International Criminal Court (ICC) can prosecute individuals for war crimes, including those committed during occupations. While the court's jurisdiction is limited to states that have ratified the Rome Statute, it demonstrates a commitment to accountability for serious breaches of international law. Moreover, the International Court of Justice (ICJ) adjudicates disputes between states and offers advisory opinions on legal questions, including those related to occupation. These judicial mechanisms are crucial for upholding the rule of law and ensuring that perpetrators are held accountable.

Non-governmental organizations (NGOs) play a significant role in monitoring human rights violations and advocating for those affected by occupations. Organisations such as Amnesty International and Human Rights Watch document abuses, raise public awareness, and lobby for international action. Their reports often inform the work of international bodies and can lead to increased pressure on occupying powers to comply with their legal obligations. Additionally, NGOs provide legal assistance to victims, helping them navigate complex legal systems and pursue justice at national and international levels.

Civil society movements also contribute to addressing violations by mobilising public opinion and pressuring governments to take action. Grassroots campaigns can draw attention to human rights abuses and advocate for policy changes both domestically and internationally. These movements often work in conjunction with international frameworks, amplifying the voices of those affected by occupation and demanding accountability. By fostering solidarity and raising awareness, civil society can play a transformative role in challenging unjust occupations and promoting adherence to international law.

Finally, national legal systems can serve as a venue for addressing violations of international law, although their effectiveness often depends on the political context. Some countries have implemented legislation that allows for the prosecution of war crimes, providing a domestic avenue for accountability. However, the willingness of national courts to act against powerful political interests can vary significantly. Strengthening the rule of law at the national level is essential for ensuring that victims have access to justice, and it complements international mechanisms by holding individuals accountable within their own jurisdictions. Together, these mechanisms create a multi-faceted approach to addressing violations of international law and human rights during occupations, reinforcing the fundamental principles of justice and accountability.

Legal recourse for victims

Legal recourse for victims of unlawful occupations is a critical aspect of international law and human rights. When a country occupies another through force, it not only violates the sovereignty of the occupied state but also endangers the rights of its citizens. These violations can include unlawful killings, forced displacement, and the deprivation of basic needs such as food, water, and medical care. Victims of such actions are entitled to seek justice and reparations under various international legal frameworks, including treaties, customary international law, and judicial bodies established to address human rights violations.

International law provides several mechanisms through which victims can pursue legal recourse. One of the primary instruments is the Geneva Conventions, which outline the responsibilities of occupying powers and the rights of individuals in occupied territories. Victims can file complaints with international bodies like the International Criminal Court (ICC) if the occupying power is a party to the Rome Statute. The ICC has jurisdiction to prosecute individuals for war crimes, including those committed during occupations, thus offering a potential avenue for accountability.

In addition to the ICC, regional human rights courts, such as the European Court of Human Rights and the Inter-American Court of Human Rights, provide platforms for victims to seek justice. These courts allow individuals to bring cases against states for human rights violations, provided they have exhausted domestic legal remedies. The decisions of these courts can lead to significant rulings that not only provide reparations to victims but also establish important precedents in international law regarding the conduct of occupying powers.

Victims may also turn to national courts to seek justice, although the effectiveness of this route can vary greatly depending on the legal framework of the occupying power. Some countries have enacted laws allowing for the prosecution of war crimes, regardless of where they occur. However, in many cases, the political climate may hinder the ability of victims to seek redress domestically. Therefore, it is essential for the international community to support efforts that empower victims to pursue justice at both national and international levels.

Finally, public awareness and advocacy play a crucial role in ensuring that victims receive the legal recourse they deserve. NGOs and human rights organisations often assist in documenting violations, providing legal aid, and raising awareness about the plight of those affected by occupation. Advocacy efforts can lead to increased pressure on occupying powers to comply with international law and can help mobilise the international community to hold violators accountable. Ultimately, the pursuit of legal recourse for victims of unlawful occupation is not only a matter of justice for individuals but also a fundamental aspect of upholding international law and human rights standards globally.

Future of international law

The future of international law, particularly in the context of occupation and human rights, is poised for significant evolution. As global dynamics shift and new conflicts emerge, the legal frameworks governing state conduct in times of occupation will likely face increased scrutiny and demand for reform. The traditional principles enshrined in treaties such as the Fourth Geneva Convention are challenged by contemporary geopolitical realities, where occupations often continue for extended periods, and the rules governing them are frequently ignored or inadequately enforced. This situation necessitates a re-examination of existing laws to ensure they adequately address the complexities of modern occupations.

One of the critical challenges facing international law is the enforcement of its provisions. While there are established legal norms that prohibit forceful occupation, such as the prohibition against the acquisition of territory by war, the mechanisms for holding violators accountable remain weak. International bodies like the United Nations have historically struggled to intervene effectively in ongoing conflicts, often hindered by political considerations among member states. The future of international law may depend on strengthening these enforcement mechanisms, potentially through the establishment of new international courts or tribunals specifically designed to address violations of occupation rights and human rights during such periods.

In addition to enforcement, the evolution of international law will likely be influenced by the increasing role of non-state actors and global civil society. Human rights organisations and grassroots movements play a crucial role in documenting violations and advocating for accountability. As technology advances, the ability to gather evidence and disseminate information about human rights abuses during occupations has improved significantly. This grassroots pressure can lead to greater international awareness and action, ultimately prompting states to adhere more closely to their legal obligations under international law.

Moreover, the intersection of international humanitarian law and human rights law will become increasingly relevant in discussions about the future of international law. While humanitarian law traditionally focuses on the conduct of hostilities, human rights law provides a broader framework for protecting individual rights at all times, including during occupations. A more integrated approach that combines these two legal domains may enhance the protection of civilians and ensure that their rights are respected, regardless of the circumstances. This holistic perspective is essential for developing a robust legal framework that addresses the realities of occupation in the modern world.

Finally, the future of international law will also be shaped by the evolving norms and values of the international community. As awareness of human rights issues grows, there is a potential for a shift in public opinion that could influence state behaviour. Countries may increasingly be held accountable not only by international bodies but also by their own citizens and global civil society. This growing expectation for compliance with international law, coupled with a commitment to human rights, could lead to significant advancements in how nations approach occupations and their responsibilities towards occupied populations. By fostering a culture of accountability and respect for the rule of law, the future of international law can contribute to a more just and equitable world.

Chapter 31: Summarising key points

The principle of self-determination is fundamental in international law, asserting that peoples have the right to freely determine their political status and pursue their economic, social, and cultural development. This principle underlies the illegality of forceful occupation, emphasising that no state has the sovereign authority to impose its will upon another through military might. The United Nations Charter explicitly prohibits the use of force against the territorial integrity or political independence of any state, framing occupation as not only a violation of sovereignty but also as a breach of international peace and security.

International law delineates clear parameters surrounding occupation, primarily established through the Hague Regulations of 1907 and the Fourth Geneva Convention of 1949. These legal frameworks outline the responsibilities of occupying powers, which include maintaining public order and safety, respecting the laws in force in the occupied territory, and ensuring the welfare of the inhabitants. Violations of these obligations can lead to accusations of war crimes, underscoring the necessity for accountability in situations of occupation. Thus, the legal landscape surrounding occupation is built on the premise that the rights and dignity of the occupied population must be preserved.

Human rights violations during occupations often manifest in various forms, including unlawful killings, torture, forced displacement, and restrictions on freedom of movement and expression. The impact on civilian populations can be devastating, leading to long-term psychological and physical harm. Reports from human rights organisations consistently document these abuses, illustrating the urgent need for international oversight and intervention. The systematic nature of these violations raises critical questions about the effectiveness of current international mechanisms in protecting human rights during periods of occupation.

The international community bears a collective responsibility to respond to and address violations of international law related to occupation. This involves not only holding offending states accountable through diplomatic channels and international courts but also supporting the rights of occupied peoples. Advocacy for stronger enforcement mechanisms and the promotion of humanitarian laws are essential steps toward ensuring that the rights of individuals are safeguarded, and that the rule of law prevails even in the most challenging contexts.

Ultimately, the discourse surrounding occupation and international law must remain dynamic and responsive to emerging challenges. The continued relevance of international law in protecting human rights during occupation is crucial in maintaining global order and justice. As such, it is imperative that both states and individuals acknowledge their roles in upholding these principles, fostering a culture of respect for international law that transcends borders and promotes peace and security for all nations.

Call to action for global awareness

The issue of occupation in international law is a pressing concern that demands global awareness and action. It is imperative to understand that international law unequivocally prohibits the forceful occupation of one country by another. Such acts violate the principles enshrined in the United Nations Charter and other international treaties designed to protect sovereignty and the rights of nations. The consequences of occupation extend beyond legal ramifications; they affect the lives of millions, leading to human rights abuses and widespread suffering.

International law provides a robust framework for addressing occupations, yet many instances of unlawful occupation persist with little consequence. The Geneva Conventions and additional protocols outline the responsibilities of occupying powers, including the obligation to protect the civilian population and uphold human rights. Violations such as forced displacement, unlawful killings, and denial of access to basic services are not mere legal infractions; they represent fundamental breaches of human dignity. It is crucial for the public to recognise these violations and understand that they must not be tolerated. Awareness can drive advocacy, compel governments to act, and press international organisations to fulfil their roles in promoting justice and accountability.

The impact of occupation is not limited to immediate human rights violations; it also has long-term repercussions on the social, economic, and political fabric of affected nations. Occupied populations often face restrictions on movement, access to education, and opportunities for economic development. This systemic disenfranchisement perpetuates cycles of poverty and conflict, creating environments where extremism can flourish. By raising awareness of these consequences, we can mobilise support for initiatives aimed at rebuilding and reconciling occupied territories. Global citizens have the power to influence policy changes and support humanitarian efforts that aim to alleviate the suffering of those living under occupation.

Advocacy for global awareness also encompasses the need for education on these issues. Schools, universities, and community organisations play a vital role in disseminating knowledge about international law and human rights. Educational programs that focus on the legality of occupations and the rights of individuals under occupation can foster a more informed citizenry. This awareness can empower individuals to take action, whether through peaceful protests, supporting humanitarian organisations, or engaging in dialogues that challenge the status quo. A well-informed public can serve as a formidable force in advocating for justice and change.

To effectively address the challenges posed by occupations, collaboration among various stakeholders is essential. Governments, civil society organisations, and international institutions must work together to promote accountability for violations of international law. Initiatives that encourage dialogue and cooperation across borders can help to bridge divides and foster mutual understanding. The call to action for global awareness is not just a plea for recognition but an urgent invitation to engage in collective efforts that uphold human rights and reinforce the rule of law. Through unity and determination, we can strive towards a world where occupations are challenged, and the rights of all individuals are respected.

Chapter 32: The Hawk's Shadow: How aggressive nations fragment World Peace

Defining hawkish nations

Hawkish nations are typically characterised by their aggressive foreign policies and a propensity to use military force to achieve their objectives. These countries prioritise military readiness and often employ a strategy of intimidation to assert their influence on the global stage. The defining traits of hawkish nations include a strong emphasis on national security, a willingness to engage in conflicts, and a belief in the necessity of military solutions to complex international issues. Such nations often perceive threats in both real and perceived forms, leading them to adopt a confrontational stance in their diplomacy and international relations.

The military strategies employed by hawkish nations are often multifaceted, incorporating both conventional and unconventional tactics. These strategies can include large-scale military buildups, aggressive posturing in international waters, and the establishment of alliances with other nations that share similar objectives. Hawkish nations may also utilise economic sanctions or cyber warfare as tools of coercion, further complicating diplomatic efforts. Such military strategies are designed not only to deter potential aggressors but also to project power and influence, often leading to escalated tensions with neighbouring states and international adversaries.

The regional conflicts that arise from hawkish diplomacy can have profound implications for global stability. When hawkish nations pursue aggressive policies, they often provoke responses from other countries, leading to a cycle of retaliation and escalating violence. This dynamic can destabilise entire regions, as smaller nations may feel compelled to align themselves with one power or another, creating polarised blocs. As these conflicts unfold, the potential for miscalculations increases, resulting in unintended consequences that further disrupt peace efforts and exacerbate humanitarian crises.

Historical case studies illustrate the impact of hawkish nations on global peace fragmentation. For instance, the actions of Nazi Germany in the 1930s serve as a stark example of how aggressive military policies can lead to widespread conflict. Similarly, the Cold War era saw the United States and the Soviet Union engage in a series of confrontations, many of which were rooted in hawkish strategies aimed at expanding their influence. These historical examples highlight the cyclical nature of aggression and conflict, demonstrating how the ambitions of one nation can ripple throughout the international system, leading to broader hostilities.

In conclusion, defining hawkish nations involves understanding their underlying motivations, military strategies, and the resulting regional conflicts that emerge from their actions. The historical context provides valuable insights into the patterns of aggression that can lead to fragmentation of world peace. As the global landscape continues to evolve, recognising and addressing the behaviours of hawkish nations will be crucial in the pursuit of sustainable peace and stability. The interplay of military power and diplomatic engagement will remain a central theme in the ongoing struggle to maintain harmony in an increasingly complex world.

The concept of World Peace

The concept of world peace has long been an aspiration for humanity, representing a state of global harmony in which nations coexist without conflict or aggression. This ideal is often envisioned as a collective effort, where countries work together to address common challenges, promote mutual understanding, and foster cooperation. However, the reality is often marred by the actions of aggressive nations, which employ hawkish strategies that undermine this aspiration. The fragmentation of world peace occurs when these nations prioritise militaristic approaches over diplomatic solutions, creating an environment of mistrust and hostility.

Aggressive hawkish nations typically engage in military strategies that prioritise force and intimidation. These strategies can manifest in various forms, including territorial expansion, military interventions, and the use of economic sanctions. Such actions not only threaten the stability of the targeted regions but also ripple outwards, affecting global peace efforts. The reliance on military might often overshadows diplomatic negotiations, as hawkish leaders may perceive military power as the most effective means of achieving their national interests. This aggressive posture can lead to an arms race, where neighbouring countries feel compelled to bolster their defences, further escalating tensions and diminishing prospects for peace.

Regional conflicts frequently arise as a direct consequence of hawkish diplomacy. When aggressive nations pursue their interests without consideration for the implications on neighbouring states, they often ignite simmering tensions into open conflicts. For instance, territorial disputes in areas like the South China Sea exemplify how the assertive actions of one nation can provoke responses from others, leading to a cycle of aggression. These regional conflicts not only destabilise the immediate area but can also draw in global powers, complicating the situation and making resolution more challenging. The inter-connectedness of modern geopolitics means that conflicts fuelled by hawkish policies can have far-reaching effects, undermining international stability.

Historical case studies reveal the patterns of aggression that contribute to the fragmentation of world peace. The Cold War serves as a prominent example, where the aggressive posturing of the United States and the Soviet Union led to a prolonged period of tension, proxy wars, and a division of the world into opposing blocs. Similarly, the actions of nations like Germany during the World Wars illustrate how aggressive nationalism can lead to catastrophic consequences, not only for the aggressor but for the entire world. These historical precedents underscore the importance of understanding the motivations behind hawkish strategies and their implications for global peace.

Ultimately, the pursuit of world peace is a complex endeavour that requires a concerted effort from all nations. It necessitates a shift away from military-centric approaches towards diplomacy, dialogue, and cooperation. The fragmentation caused by aggressive nations serves as a poignant reminder of the fragility of peace and the need for a collective commitment to addressing the root causes of conflict. By recognising the detrimental effects of hawkish policies and fostering an environment conducive to understanding and collaboration, the international community can work towards a more peaceful future.

Chapter 33: The characteristics of aggressive nations

Aggression in international relations refers to the use of military force or coercive diplomacy by a state to achieve its goals, often at the expense of another state's sovereignty. This behaviour is typically characterised by an imbalance of power, where the aggressor seeks to impose its will on a weaker state or group. Understanding aggression requires analysing both the motivations behind such actions and their implications for global stability. Factors such as national interest, economic gain, and ideological dominance often drive these aggressive actions, leading to a cycle of conflict that can destabilise entire regions.

The concept of aggressive nations is often linked to hawkish military strategies that prioritise the use of force over diplomacy. Hawkish nations typically perceive military power as a primary tool for achieving their objectives, which can manifest in various forms, including direct military intervention, threats of force, or the establishment of military alliances aimed at deterring opposition. This approach to foreign policy not only reflects a national ethos that values strength but also perpetuates a culture of fear and mistrust among nations. As a result, aggressive military strategies can lead to an arms race, where nations feel compelled to expand their own military capabilities in response to perceived threats.

Regional conflicts frequently arise from the aggressive diplomacy of hawkish nations. When a state adopts a confrontational stance, it can provoke responses from neighbouring countries that feel threatened or marginalised. These tensions can escalate into armed conflicts, which not only disrupt regional stability but also have far-reaching consequences on a global scale. For instance, the actions of a hawkish nation can create refugee crises, economic instability, and humanitarian emergencies, further exacerbating the fragmentation of international peace. Thus, the aggressive posturing of one state can have a domino effect, destabilising entire regions and prompting a cycle of retaliation and conflict.

Historical case studies provide valuable insights into how aggression shapes international relations and contributes to the fragmentation of peace. Events such as the invasion of Iraq in 2003 or Russia's annexation of Crimea in 2014 illustrate how aggressive actions can lead to widespread condemnation, economic sanctions, and military responses from other nations. These incidents highlight the complexities of international law and the challenges of maintaining a rules-based order in the face of aggression. The consequences of such actions often extend beyond immediate military conflicts, influencing global political dynamics and altering alliances for years to come.

In conclusion, defining aggression in international relations involves understanding the motivations, strategies, and consequences of hawkish behaviour. Aggressive nations, through their military strategies and diplomatic posturing, contribute to the fragmentation of world peace by inciting regional conflicts and fostering an atmosphere of distrust. As the world grapples with the realities of international aggression, it becomes increasingly essential to seek comprehensive strategies that prioritise peace and security over military confrontation.

Political and military traits of hawkish nations

Hawkish nations often exhibit distinct political and military traits that contribute to their aggressive posture on the world stage. Politically, these countries tend to prioritise national security and defence over diplomatic solutions, frequently adopting a belligerent stance in international relations. Their leadership often relies on militaristic rhetoric, framing foreign policy decisions in terms of threats to national sovereignty and survival. This mindset fosters an environment where military action is viewed as a viable solution to conflicts, leading to a propensity for interventionist policies that can destabilise regional and global peace.

Militarily, hawkish nations typically maintain robust armed forces and invest heavily in defence spending. This emphasis on military readiness is often justified by perceived threats from rival states or non-state actors. Such nations might prioritise the development of advanced weaponry and military technology, seeking to maintain a strategic advantage. This dynamic can create a cycle of tension and mistrust, further undermining prospects for peaceful resolution of conflicts.

Regional conflicts frequently arise as a direct consequence of hawkish diplomacy. These nations may engage in aggressive posturing or military interventions that provoke retaliatory actions from other countries. The resulting conflicts can escalate quickly, drawing in multiple parties and complicating diplomatic efforts. For instance, interventions in civil wars or territorial disputes often exacerbate existing tensions, leading to prolonged instability. The involvement of hawkish nations can also polarise regional actors, as alliances form around opposing sides, making it increasingly difficult to achieve a consensus for peace.

Historical case studies illustrate the consequences of aggressive policies adopted by hawkish nations. The United States' involvement in Vietnam and Iraq serves as prominent examples where military intervention led to significant loss of life, regional instability, and long-term ramifications for global peace. Similarly, Russia's annexation of Crimea and military involvement in Ukraine exemplify how hawkish strategies can result in widespread conflict and international condemnation. These instances highlight the fragility of peace in the face of militaristic approaches, emphasising the potential for hawkish nations to fragment rather than foster stability.

Ultimately, the political and military traits of hawkish nations contribute to a landscape where peace is continually threatened by aggression and conflict. The focus on military solutions over diplomatic dialogue creates a cycle of hostility that can engulf entire regions. Understanding these traits is essential for policymakers and global citizens alike, as it underscores the importance of pursuing peaceful solutions and fostering dialogue in an increasingly polarised world. Only through a comprehensive understanding of the dynamics at play can efforts be made to mitigate the fragmentation of world peace caused by hawkish nations.

The role of nationalism and militarism

Nationalism and militarism play pivotal roles in shaping the actions and policies of aggressive nations, often leading to fragmentation of world peace. Nationalism, characterised by a strong identification with one's nation and the promotion of its interests above those of others, fuels a sense of superiority and entitlement among its proponents. This fervent loyalty can drive nations to adopt aggressive foreign policies, as leaders harness nationalist sentiments to justify military actions. Militarism, the belief in the maintenance of a strong military and readiness to use it aggressively, complements nationalism by providing the means with which these aggressive ambitions can be pursued. Together, these ideologies create a formidable force that can destabilise international relations and escalate conflicts.

Aggressive hawkish nations often employ military strategies that reflect their nationalist fervour and militaristic tendencies. These strategies include pre-emptive strikes, military interventions, and the establishment of military alliances aimed at expanding territorial claims or asserting dominance over regional rivals. The underlying belief is that military strength not only secures national interests but also acts as a deterrent against potential adversaries. The cycle of aggression and militarisation is self-perpetuating, as each act of hostility invites retaliation and countermeasures.

Diplomatic relations can become strained when countries prioritise military might over dialogue, leading to misunderstandings and escalating tensions. In regions where aggressive nations exert their influence, smaller states may feel threatened and compelled to align with other powers for protection, resulting in a web of alliances that complicates conflict resolution. The situations in Eastern Europe, the South China Sea, and the Middle East exemplify how hawkish diplomacy can create volatile environments where peace is precarious, and conflicts can ignite with little warning.

Historical case studies provide valuable insights into the consequences of nationalism and militarism on global peace. The lead-up to World War I is a prime example, where nationalist fervour and militaristic posturing among European powers contributed to a catastrophic conflict. Similarly, the rise of militaristic regimes in the 20th century, such as Nazi Germany and Imperial Japan, showcased how aggressive nationalism could lead to widespread devastation. In more recent history, the invasions of Iraq and Afghanistan by the United States demonstrate how a combination of national interest and military might can result in prolonged conflict and instability, undermining global peace efforts.

The interplay between nationalism, militarism, and international relations underscores the fragility of world peace. As aggressive nations continue to prioritise military solutions over diplomacy, the potential for conflict remains high. Understanding the role of these ideologies is crucial for policymakers and citizens alike, as it highlights the need for a balanced approach that prioritises dialogue and cooperation over aggression. Fostering an environment where peace is valued and military solutions are seen as a last resort is essential to countering the fragmentation of world peace caused by hawkish nations.

Chapter 34: Military Strategies of Hawkish Nations

Types of military strategies

Military strategies employed by aggressive nations can significantly influence global stability and contribute to the fragmentation of world peace. These strategies often reflect a nation's geopolitical ambitions, historical context, and economic interests. Understanding the various types of military strategies is crucial for comprehending how hawkish nations operate and the implications of their actions on regional and global peace. The primary types of military strategies include deterrence, compellence, and preventive warfare, each with its distinct characteristics and objectives.

Deterrence strategy relies on the threat of significant retaliation to prevent adversaries from taking aggressive actions. This approach is commonly seen in nuclear-armed states, where the possession of powerful weapons serves as a means of discouragement. Countries employing deterrence often maintain a robust military presence and engage in military exercises to demonstrate their capabilities. This strategy, while effective in some contexts, can also lead to arms races and increased tensions, as nations feel compelled to enhance their own military capabilities in response to perceived threats.

Compellence, on the other hand, aims to force an adversary to take a specific action, such as withdrawing from a territory or altering a policy. This strategy can be direct, involving military threats or actual force, or indirect, using economic sanctions and diplomatic pressure. Aggressive nations often resort to compellence in regional conflicts to achieve short-term objectives quickly. However, the use of compellence can backfire, as it may lead to prolonged conflicts and resistance from the targeted states, ultimately exacerbating tensions and undermining peace efforts.

Preventive warfare is a more controversial strategy that involves taking military action against a perceived threat before it materialises. This pre-emptive approach is based on the belief that waiting for an adversary to strike first could result in greater losses. Countries that adopt preventive warfare often justify their actions as necessary for national security, claiming that they are acting in self-defence. However, this strategy can lead to significant instability, as it may provoke retaliatory actions and create a cycle of violence that further fragments international relations.

In addition to these strategies, it is essential to consider the historical context of aggressive nations and their military approaches. Case studies, such as the invasions of Iraq and Afghanistan, illustrate how aggressive military strategies can lead to unintended consequences, including regional destabilisation and humanitarian crises. The actions of hawkish nations not only impact their immediate adversaries but also ripple through the international system, affecting alliances and global power dynamics. Understanding these military strategies and their implications is vital for addressing the challenges posed by aggressive nations and fostering a more peaceful world.

The Doctrine of pre-emptive strikes

The doctrine of pre-emptive strikes has emerged as a significant military strategy embraced by aggressive nations seeking to assert their influence and safeguard their interests. This approach involves launching an attack against a perceived threat before that threat can materialise. By adopting this strategy, hawkish nations justify military actions not only as defensive measures but also as a means to maintain dominance in volatile regions. The rationale behind pre-emptive strikes often stems from a belief that waiting for an adversary to act could lead to catastrophic consequences, thereby legitimising the use of force in the name of national security.

Historically, the application of pre-emptive strikes has had profound implications for international relations, often leading to fragmentation of world peace. One of the most notable examples is Israel's attack on Egypt in 1967, which initiated the Six-Day War. Israel perceived an imminent threat from neighbouring Arab states, prompting a pre-emptive strike that redefined the geopolitical landscape in the Middle East. This military action, while successful in achieving immediate objectives, escalated regional tensions and fostered a cycle of conflict that has persisted for decades. Such incidents illustrate how the doctrine can lead to prolonged instability and disrupt diplomatic efforts aimed at conflict resolution.

The consequences of pre-emptive strikes extend beyond immediate military outcomes; they can severely impact regional dynamics and international alliances. Nations that adopt aggressive postures risk alienating potential allies and fostering animosity among neighbouring states. For instance, the United States' decision to invade Iraq in 2003 was justified through a pre-emptive strategy aimed at neutralising a perceived threat from weapons of mass destruction. The aftermath of this action not only destabilised Iraq but also strained relationships with other nations, leading to a fragmented Middle Eastern landscape characterised by ongoing violence and mistrust.

Furthermore, the doctrine of pre-emptive strikes contributes to an arms race, as nations feel compelled to enhance their military capabilities in response to perceived threats. This escalation creates an environment of fear and suspicion, where the potential for conflict increases. As countries invest in advanced weaponry and military infrastructure, the focus shifts away from diplomatic engagement and conflict resolution, further fragmenting global peace efforts. The cycle of aggression and defence becomes self-perpetuating, making it increasingly challenging to foster cooperative international relations.

In conclusion, the doctrine of pre-emptive strikes represents a critical aspect of hawkish military strategies that contribute to the fragmentation of world peace. By prioritising aggressive actions over diplomatic resolutions, nations that adopt this doctrine not only risk prolonged conflict but also undermine the very foundations of international cooperation. Understanding the historical implications and contemporary consequences of such strategies is essential for recognising the challenges facing global peace in an increasingly polarised world. Addressing these issues requires a concerted effort to promote dialogue, build trust, and seek alternatives to military confrontation.

Proxy wars and their implications

Proxy wars have emerged as a significant tool for aggressive nations seeking to extend their influence without direct confrontation. These conflicts, often fought in third-party countries, allow hawkish nations to engage in military strategies that serve their geopolitical interests while minimising the risks and costs associated with traditional warfare. By supporting local factions or rebel groups, these nations can destabilise regions, project power, and achieve strategic objectives, all while maintaining the facade of non-involvement. The implications of such tactics are profound, as they contribute to the fragmentation of world peace and escalate tensions on a global scale.

The motivations for engaging in proxy wars are often rooted in a desire for regional dominance or the containment of rival powers. For instance, during the Cold War, the United States and the Soviet Union supported opposing sides in various conflicts, from Korea to Vietnam, aiming to prevent the spread of each other's ideologies. This approach not only prolonged conflicts but also led to humanitarian crises and the destabilisation of entire regions. Today, similar dynamics can be observed in conflicts such as those in Syria and Ukraine, where major powers leverage local actors to further their own interests, often at the expense of civilian populations and national sovereignty.

The military strategies employed in proxy wars are varied and complex. Aggressive nations may provide financial support, weapons, and training to their chosen allies, effectively turning local conflicts into battlegrounds for larger geopolitical struggles. These strategies often lead to an escalation of violence, as local factions become heavily armed and increasingly reliant on external support. The consequences are dire, resulting in prolonged violence, destruction of infrastructure, and significant loss of life. Additionally, the involvement of multiple external actors can complicate peace negotiations, creating a web of interests that makes resolution increasingly difficult.

Regional conflicts stemming from hawkish diplomacy can have far-reaching implications beyond the immediate area of conflict. The spillover effects can destabilise neighbouring countries, leading to refugee crises, economic turmoil, and even the spread of extremist ideologies. For example, the Syrian civil war has not only caused millions to flee their homes but has also influenced political dynamics in Europe and the Middle East. Such conflicts exacerbate existing tensions, leading to a cycle of violence that further fragments the potential for lasting peace and cooperation among nations.

Historical case studies illustrate the detrimental effects of proxy wars on global peace. The Vietnam War serves as a prime example where U.S. involvement, framed as a fight against communism, resulted in immense suffering and a long-lasting impact on both Vietnam and U.S. foreign policy. Similarly, the ongoing conflict in Afghanistan, characterised by foreign intervention and support for various factions, reflects the complexities and unintended consequences of proxy warfare. These examples underscore the urgent need for a revaluation of military strategies employed by aggressive nations, emphasising diplomacy and collaboration over confrontation to foster a more stable and peaceful world.

Chapter 35: The influence of hawkish diplomacy

Diplomatic tactics of aggressive nations

Diplomatic tactics employed by aggressive nations often serve as a façade that conceals underlying militaristic ambitions. These nations leverage diplomacy not merely as a tool for negotiation but as a means to further their strategic objectives, often at the expense of global stability. By presenting themselves as reasonable actors in the international arena, hawkish nations can distract from their aggressive posturing, manipulate perceptions, and create a narrative that justifies their actions. This duality complicates international relations and creates an environment ripe for conflict, as other nations may find it challenging to discern genuine intentions from deceptive rhetoric.

One common tactic used by aggressive nations is the employment of coercive diplomacy, where threats and ultimatums are used to compel compliance from weaker states. This approach often involves a combination of military posturing and economic pressure, leading to a chilling effect on diplomatic negotiations. For instance, when a nation amasses troops along a border while simultaneously demanding concessions from its neighbour, it creates a precarious situation where the threatened state may feel forced to acquiesce, thereby undermining the principles of sovereignty and mutual respect that are foundational to international diplomacy.

Another strategy involves the manipulation of international institutions and treaties to legitimise aggressive actions. Nations that engage in hawkish diplomacy often seek to position themselves as defenders of international law while simultaneously violating it. By framing their actions within the context of self-defence or humanitarian intervention, they can garner support or at least neutrality from other countries. This tactic can lead to a fragmentation of global consensus, as nations become divided over the interpretation of international norms, making it increasingly difficult to achieve collective action against aggression.

Regional conflicts frequently arise from the aggressive diplomatic manoeuvres of hawkish nations, as their actions can instigate rivalries and escalate tensions among neighbouring states. The use of proxy conflicts is a hallmark of such tactics, allowing aggressive nations to exert influence without direct involvement. This can destabilise entire regions, as local actors become embroiled in the larger geopolitical games being played. Consequently, the resulting fragmentation of peace is often marked by prolonged violence, humanitarian crises, and the erosion of trust among states that could otherwise collaborate on shared challenges.

Historical case studies vividly illustrate the consequences of aggressive diplomacy. The behaviour of nations during the Cold War exemplifies how hawkish tactics can lead to significant geopolitical fragmentation. The arms race, coupled with the establishment of opposing alliances, demonstrated how aggressive posturing could not only divide nations but also create a climate of suspicion and hostility that persisted for decades. Similar patterns can be observed in more contemporary conflicts, where the diplomatic strategies of aggressive nations continue to challenge the fragile fabric of international peace, highlighting the urgent need for a revaluation of how diplomacy is conducted in an increasingly polarised world.

The role of alliances and coalitions

The dynamics of international relations often hinge on the formation and sustainability of alliances and coalitions, which can significantly influence global peace efforts. In the context of aggressive hawkish nations, these alliances serve dual purposes: they can bolster military strategies and create a united front against perceived threats, but they can also lead to increased tensions and fragmentation of peace. As nations align themselves with others that share similar aggressive tendencies, the potential for conflict escalates, complicating diplomatic efforts and undermining the foundations of global stability.

Alliances among hawkish nations are frequently characterised by a mutual interest in asserting military dominance. Such relationships can manifest through formal treaties or informal partnerships, where nations collaborate on defence strategies, share intelligence, and conduct joint military exercises. These actions not only enhance their collective military capabilities but also signal to the international community their readiness to confront challenges through force. However, this militarisation can provoke fear and resistance from other nations, leading to an arms race that further destabilises the region and diminishes the prospects for peaceful resolutions.

The formation of coalitions often reflects a response to regional conflicts, where aggressive nations seek to consolidate power or influence over contested areas. For instance, historical case studies reveal that countries with expansionist agendas frequently form coalitions to legitimise their actions, portraying them as collective security measures rather than acts of aggression. Such coalitions can exacerbate existing tensions, resulting in a cycle of retaliation and conflict that fragments peace efforts. The collective military posturing can alienate nations that may have otherwise been neutral, pushing them to form counter-coalitions and perpetuating a cycle of hostility.

Moreover, the impact of these alliances extends beyond immediate military considerations. The economic and political dimensions of coalition-building often lead to the establishment of spheres of influence, where aggressive nations impose their will on weaker states. This dynamic can create a hierarchy that undermines the sovereignty of smaller nations, which may feel compelled to align with stronger powers for their own security. In time, this can lead to widespread resentment and resistance, further eroding trust among nations and complicating diplomatic relations.

Ultimately, the role of alliances and coalitions among aggressive nations illustrates a paradox in international relations: while they may provide a sense of security and strength to their members, they simultaneously contribute to the fragmentation of world peace. As aggressive nations continue to pursue their interests through military alliances, the potential for misunderstanding and conflict increases. The challenge for the international community lies in addressing these dynamics, promoting dialogue, and fostering cooperative frameworks that prioritise peace over aggression, thereby reducing the likelihood of conflict and fragmentation in an increasingly polarised world.

Economic sanctions and military aid

Economic sanctions and military aid are two powerful tools often employed by nations to exert influence and shape the geopolitical landscape. These measures are frequently used in tandem, with sanctions aimed at crippling an adversary's economy while military aid is provided to allies or proxy forces to bolster their capabilities. The interplay between these two strategies can have profound implications for international relations and regional stability, particularly in contexts where aggressive nations seek to assert their dominance.

Economic sanctions are typically imposed by one or more countries to compel a change in behaviour from a target state. These sanctions can take various forms, including trade restrictions, asset freezes, and financial embargoes. While the intention behind sanctions may be to deter aggressive actions or encourage compliance with international norms, their effectiveness is often debated. In many cases, sanctions can exacerbate existing tensions, leading to a cycle of hostility and retaliation that undermines peace efforts. Aggressive nations may find ways to circumvent sanctions, prompting further escalations and complicating diplomatic resolutions.

Conversely, military aid serves as a means of supporting allies and countering the influence of adversarial states. By providing weapons, training, and logistical support, nations can enhance the military capabilities of their partners, thereby shifting the balance of power in a region. However, this assistance can also fuel conflicts, as rival nations perceive the bolstered strength of their opponents as a direct threat. The resulting arms races can provoke aggressive posturing and lead to heightened tensions, which often detracts from efforts to achieve long-term peace.

Historical case studies illustrate the complexities surrounding economic sanctions and military aid. The United States has employed both strategies in various conflicts, from the sanctions against Iraq in the 1990s to military support for Ukraine in the face of Russian aggression. Each instance highlights the delicate balance between applying pressure on aggressive nations and providing support to vulnerable allies. The unintended consequences of these actions can lead to fragmentation of peace, as regional actors respond to perceived threats with their own military buildups or alliances, often resulting in a destabilising feedback loop.

Ultimately, the relationship between economic sanctions and military aid is a double-edged sword in the realm of international diplomacy. While these measures can serve as deterrents against aggression, they can also precipitate a cycle of conflict and mistrust. Understanding the dynamics of this interplay is essential for policymakers aiming to navigate the complex landscape of global relations and foster a more stable and peaceful world. As aggressive hawkish nations continue to challenge the status quo, the careful calibration of sanctions and military support will remain a critical component of any strategy aimed at preserving peace.

Chapter 36: Regional conflicts stemming from hawkish diplomacy

C ase study: The Middle East
The Middle East serves as a critical case study in understanding how aggressive nations contribute to the fragmentation of world peace. The region has long been a focal point for geopolitical struggles, with various nations pursuing hawkish policies that exacerbate tensions and conflict. Historical events, such as the Arab-Israeli conflict, the Gulf Wars, and the ongoing Syrian civil war, illustrate how aggressive military strategies and diplomatic posturing can destabilise entire regions and provoke broader international ramifications.

One of the most significant examples of hawkish diplomacy in the Middle East can be traced back to the establishment of Israel in 1948. The ensuing Arab-Israeli conflict created a series of military confrontations and territorial disputes, fuelled by nationalist sentiments and reinforced by external powers. Nations such as the United States and the Soviet Union, each supporting different sides, intensified the conflict further through military aid and strategic alliances. This intervention not only entrenched hostilities but also led to a cycle of violence that perpetuated instability and fragmented peace efforts in the region.

In more recent years, the U.S.-led invasion of Iraq in 2003 exemplifies how aggressive military strategies can lead to unforeseen consequences. The removal of Saddam Hussein's regime created a power vacuum, resulting in sectarian violence and the rise of extremist groups such as ISIS. This intervention was justified under the pretext of promoting democracy and stability, yet it instead contributed to widespread chaos, highlighting the pitfalls of hawkish strategies that disregard the complex social and political fabric of the region. The fallout from this invasion continues to affect regional dynamics, prompting further military responses from various nations as they seek to counteract the repercussions of earlier interventions.

Moreover, the ongoing civil war in Syria has become a stage for various aggressive nations to pursue their interests, complicating the already fragile peace landscape. Multiple actors, including Russia, Iran, and Turkey, have engaged in military operations under the guise of protecting national interests or supporting specific factions. This external involvement has not only prolonged the conflict but also generated a humanitarian crisis, displacing millions and leading to increased tensions among neighbouring countries. The Syrian situation exemplifies how hawkish diplomacy can escalate conflicts, undermining diplomatic resolutions and fragmenting peace efforts.

In conclusion, the Middle East serves as a stark reminder of how aggressive nations can fragment world peace through military strategies and hawkish diplomacy. The historical case studies of the Arab-Israeli conflict, the Iraq War, and the Syrian civil war reveal a pattern of intervention that often fails to consider the long-term implications for regional stability. As nations continue to pursue aggressive policies, the lessons from the Middle East underscore the need for a more cooperative and diplomatic approach to international relations, one that prioritises peace over military might.

Case study: Eastern Europe

In Eastern Europe, the resurgence of aggressive nationalism and military posturing has significantly contributed to the fragmentation of regional peace. This subchapter examines the historical and contemporary dynamics that have shaped the geopolitical landscape of Eastern Europe, focusing on how hawkish nations have exploited ethnic divisions and historical grievances to assert dominance. The case of Russia's actions in Ukraine serves as a pivotal example of how aggressive foreign policies can destabilise entire regions and incite conflicts that resonate globally.

The annexation of Crimea in 2014 marked a critical juncture in Eastern European geopolitics, illustrating the direct impact of hawkish policies on regional stability. Russia's justification for this military intervention was rooted in the protection of ethnic Russians and Russian speakers in Ukraine. This narrative conveniently overlooked Ukraine's sovereignty and the rights of its citizens, leading to widespread condemnation from the international community. The consequences were swift, as the conflict escalated into a protracted war in the Donbas region, entrenching divisions not only within Ukraine but also across Eastern Europe, as neighbouring states grappled with the implications of Russian aggression.

In the wake of these developments, the response from NATO and the European Union has been a mixture of deterrence and diplomacy. While military exercises and increased troop deployments in Eastern European member states aimed to bolster security, they also risked exacerbating tensions with Russia. This dual approach reflects the challenges of maintaining peace in a region where aggressive strategies are often met with militarised responses, leading to a cycle of provocation and counter-provocation. Countries like Poland and the Baltic states have found themselves in a precarious position, caught between their desire for security and the need to avoid escalating conflicts with their powerful neighbour.

The fragmentation of Eastern European peace is further complicated by internal divisions within nations, where hawkish rhetoric can influence political discourse and exacerbate ethnic tensions. In countries such as Hungary and Romania, nationalist sentiments have risen, often intertwined with historical grievances related to territorial disputes and minority rights. These internal dynamics underscore the fragility of peace in the region, as governments may exploit nationalist sentiments to consolidate power, thereby diverting attention from pressing socio-economic issues and fostering environments ripe for conflict.

Ultimately, the case study of Eastern Europe underscores the critical need for comprehensive strategies that address the root causes of aggression and fragmentation. Diplomatic engagement, coupled with robust support for democratic institutions and civil society, is essential to counteract the influence of hawkish nations. Only through a concerted effort to promote dialogue and understanding can the international community hope to mitigate the risks posed by aggressive nationalism and foster a sustainable path toward peace in a region still haunted by the shadows of its turbulent past.

Case study: The Asia-Pacific region

The Asia-Pacific region stands as a complex tapestry of geopolitical tensions and historical grievances, where aggressive nations have significantly contributed to the fragmentation of world peace. This landscape is characterised by a myriad of conflicts fuelled by national interests, territorial disputes, and the relentless pursuit of military superiority. Countries such as China, North Korea, and to some extent, the United States, have adopted hawkish stances that exacerbate regional tensions, often leading to confrontations that threaten broader global stability.

One of the most salient examples of hawkish diplomacy in the Asia-Pacific is China's assertiveness in the South China Sea. The region is rich in resources and strategically significant for global shipping routes, making it a focal point for territorial claims. China's militarisation of artificial islands and its aggressive stance against neighbouring nations such as Vietnam and the Philippines have heightened tensions, prompting military buildups and alliances among those nations. This behaviour exemplifies how aggressive policies can lead to an arms race and increased instability, undermining diplomatic efforts aimed at peaceful resolutions.

North Korea's military strategies further illustrate the fragmentation of peace in the region. The country, under Kim Jong-un's leadership, has pursued a nuclear weapons program that defies international norms and provokes widespread condemnation. Pyongyang's provocative missile tests and threats against South Korea and the United States serve to heighten fears of conflict, leading to a cycle of escalation. These actions not only strain bilateral relations but also compel neighbouring countries to bolster their defences, thereby perpetuating a climate of mistrust and hostility.

The historical context of these tensions reveals a legacy of aggressive expansionism and imperialism that continues to shape current dynamics. For instance, Japan's militaristic past and the scars of World War II still influence its relations with China and Korea. Similarly, the United States' interventions in the region, from the Korean War to its ongoing military presence in various countries, have often been perceived as acts of aggression, leading to deep-seated resentments. This historical backdrop complicates diplomatic efforts and fosters a fragmented peace, where old wounds are reopened by hawkish rhetoric and military posturing.

In conclusion, the Asia-Pacific region serves as a critical case study in understanding how aggressive nations contribute to the fragmentation of world peace. The interplay of military strategies, historical grievances, and hawkish diplomacy creates an environment ripe for conflict. As nations engage in competitive posturing and military buildups, the prospect of achieving lasting peace diminishes. Acknowledging these dynamics is essential for policymakers and scholars alike, as they seek to navigate the complexities of international relations in a region fraught with tension and potential for conflict.

Chapter 37: Historical case studies of aggressive nations

The rise of Nazi Germany

The rise of Nazi Germany in the early 20th century serves as a pivotal case study in understanding how aggressive nations can fragment world peace. After World War I, Germany faced significant economic hardship and political instability, largely due to the Treaty of Versailles. This treaty not only imposed heavy reparations on Germany but also stripped it of territories and military capabilities. The resultant discontent created fertile ground for extremist ideologies to take root, allowing Adolf Hitler and the National Socialist German Workers' Party (NSDAP) to gain popularity by promising national rejuvenation and the restoration of German pride.

Hitler's ascent to power in 1933 marked the beginning of an aggressive foreign policy that aimed to overturn the post-World War I settlement. By leveraging economic turmoil, social unrest, and nationalist sentiments, the Nazi regime positioned itself as the saviour of a beleaguered nation. The regime's militarisation and expansionist ambitions were not merely reactive; they were a fundamental component of its ideology, which sought to establish a Greater Germany through the annexation of territories inhabited by ethnic Germans and the subjugation of perceived inferior races.

The implementation of aggressive military strategies illustrated the regime's commitment to its expansionist goals. The remilitarisation of the Rhineland in 1936, the annexation of Austria in 1938, and the subsequent dismemberment of Czechoslovakia through the Munich Agreement showcased a pattern of bluff and intimidation that caught European powers off guard. Rather than fostering diplomatic solutions, these actions exacerbated tensions across the continent, leading to a fragmented diplomatic landscape. The failure of appeasement strategies further emboldened Hitler, illustrating how aggressive nations can exploit the desire for peace to pursue their objectives unchecked.

As Nazi Germany continued its expansion, the implications for regional stability were profound. The invasion of Poland in September 1939 not only triggered World War II but also revealed the catastrophic consequences of unchecked aggressive diplomacy. The resulting conflict engulfed Europe and beyond, leading to unprecedented levels of destruction and loss of life. This scenario exemplifies how aggressive nations, through military posturing and the violation of international norms, can destabilise regional and global peace, creating a legacy of conflict that resonates to this day.

The historical case of Nazi Germany underscores the critical lessons regarding the relationship between aggressive nations and world peace. It highlights the need for robust international frameworks and collective security measures to deter expansionist ambitions. The fragmentation of peace resulting from Nazi aggression serves as a cautionary tale for contemporary global politics, reminding us of the importance of vigilance against hawkish nationalism and the necessity of fostering cooperative diplomatic relations to prevent the re-emergence of similar threats.

THE COLD WAR AND SOVIET expansionism

The cold war marked a significant period of geopolitical tension between the Soviet Union and the Western powers, particularly the United States, following World War II. This era was characterised by an intense ideological struggle between communism and capitalism, leading to various strategies employed by the Soviet Union to expand its influence across Eastern Europe and beyond. Soviet expansionism during this time was not merely a quest for territorial gain but rather a calculated effort to promote communist ideology and counter Western influence, which the USSR perceived as a direct threat to its existence.

In Eastern Europe, the Soviet Union established a sphere of influence that included countries such as Poland, Hungary, and Czechoslovakia. The imposition of communist regimes in these nations was often executed through military intervention or political coercion. This strategy solidified a buffer zone against the West and facilitated the spread of Soviet-style governance, which sought to align these nations with Moscow's political and ideological directives. The establishment of the Warsaw Pact in 1955 further institutionalised this bloc, fostering military cooperation among the Eastern European states and presenting a unified front against NATO.

The Korean War exemplified the global ramifications of Soviet expansionism, as it was a direct manifestation of Cold War tensions. The conflict, which erupted in 1950, saw the North, backed by the USSR and China, clash with the South, supported by United Nations forces led by the United States. This war highlighted how the ideological battle between communism and democracy could spiral into military conflicts, resulting in significant loss of life and further entrenchment of hostilities between the superpowers. The Korean Peninsula remains divided to this day, a testament to the lasting impact of Cold War dynamics.

The Soviet Union's aggressive foreign policy also led to significant regional conflicts in places such as Vietnam and Afghanistan. In Vietnam, the U.S. intervention aimed to prevent the spread of communism, which was viewed as a direct threat to global stability. The resulting conflict not only devastated Vietnam but also deepened the divisions within the United States and its allies. Similarly, the Soviet invasion of Afghanistan in 1979 aimed at bolstering a communist regime, but instead ignited a protracted and costly war that drained Soviet resources and contributed to the eventual dissolution of the USSR.

In conclusion, the Cold War era was marked by Soviet expansionism that sought to reshape the geopolitical landscape through aggressive and often destabilising strategies. The ideological battle between communism and capitalism resulted in numerous regional conflicts, which fragmented global peace and led to a legacy of mistrust and rivalry. Understanding the historical context of this period is crucial in analysing how aggressive nations can influence international relations and contribute to the fragmentation of world peace. The lessons learned from the Cold War continue to resonate in contemporary geopolitical conflicts, reminding us of the delicate balance between power, ideology, and stability.

Recent aggressions: Russia and China

Recent years have witnessed a notable escalation in aggressive posturing and actions by both Russia and China, raising significant concerns about global peace and security. The annexation of Crimea by Russia in 2014 marked a critical turning point, as it not only challenged international norms but also set a precedent for military aggression in Europe. This move was accompanied by military exercises and a sustained presence in Eastern Ukraine, where Russia has been accused of supporting separatist movements. Similarly, China's assertive claims over the South China Sea and its militarisation of artificial islands signify a strategic pivot that threatens regional stability and challenges the influence of neighbouring states and the United States.

The military strategies employed by both nations reflect a blend of traditional and hybrid warfare tactics designed to project power while minimising direct confrontation with Western nations. Russia has effectively utilised cyber warfare, disinformation campaigns, and proxy conflicts to extend its influence without resorting to overt military engagement. This approach allows Russia to exploit vulnerabilities in democratic societies, destabilising them from within. On the other hand, China's strategy emphasises economic leverage alongside military modernisation, which includes the development of advanced naval capabilities and missile systems. This dual approach aims to assert dominance in key regions while fostering dependency through economic ties.

Regional conflicts stemming from the aggressive diplomacy of Russia and China have led to a fragmentation of alliances and a re-evaluation of security strategies among affected nations. In Eastern Europe, NATO has increased its presence in response to Russian threats, leading to heightened tensions between Moscow and the West. In Asia, countries such as Japan, India, and Australia are recalibrating their defence policies to counterbalance China's growing assertiveness. The resulting arms race and the formation of new strategic partnerships illustrate how aggressive postures can catalyse an environment of mistrust and hostility, further complicating the prospects for peace.

Historical case studies provide critical insights into the patterns and consequences of aggressive actions by nations. The Cold War era serves as a poignant example, where the U.S. and the Soviet Union engaged in a prolonged period of military and ideological conflict that fragmented global alliances and sparked numerous proxy wars. Similarly, the rise of Nazi Germany illustrates how unchecked aggression can lead to catastrophic wars and widespread destruction. These historical precedents underscore the importance of understanding the motivations behind aggressive actions and the potential repercussions for global stability.

As the international community grapples with the implications of recent aggressions by Russia and China, it becomes imperative to foster dialogue and collaborative security measures. Diplomatic efforts must be reinforced to counteract the fragmentation caused by hawkish policies, emphasising conflict resolution and mutual understanding. Additionally, international organisations should play a more assertive role in addressing these conflicts, as a unified response is essential to mitigating the risks posed by aggressive nations. Without such efforts, the cycle of aggression and fragmentation is likely to continue, threatening the foundational principles of global peace and security.

Chapter 38: The consequences of fragmented peace

Humanitarian impacts of conflict
    Humanitarian impacts of conflict are profound and multifaceted, significantly affecting the lives of civilians caught in the crossfire of aggressive military strategies employed by hawkish nations. The repercussions extend beyond immediate physical danger, manifesting in long-term psychological trauma, displacement, and the collapse of social structures. Civilians often bear the brunt of military actions, facing violence, loss of livelihood, and the erosion of basic human rights. The deliberate targeting of civilian populations, as seen in various conflicts, not only compounds suffering but also exacerbates social divisions and hinders post-conflict recovery efforts.

Displacement is one of the most visible humanitarian impacts of conflict, with millions forced to flee their homes due to violence and insecurity. Internally displaced persons (IDPs) and refugees face numerous challenges, including inadequate access to food, clean water, and medical care. The influx of refugees into neighbouring countries can strain local resources, leading to tensions between host communities and newcomers. This dynamic often creates a cycle of conflict where humanitarian needs are overshadowed by rising nationalism and xenophobia, further complicating efforts to maintain peace and stability in the region.

Survivors of violence may experience post-traumatic stress disorder (PTSD), depression, and anxiety, affecting their ability to rebuild their lives. Children, in particular, are vulnerable to these effects, as exposure to violence can hinder their development and education. The loss of educational opportunities perpetuates a cycle of poverty and instability, as future generations are deprived of the skills necessary to contribute positively to society. As hawkish policies lead to ongoing conflict, the humanitarian impacts become intergenerational, creating a landscape of despair that is difficult to escape.

Healthcare systems often collapse in conflict zones, leading to widespread health crises. The destruction of infrastructure, coupled with the targeting of medical facilities, results in a lack of access to essential health services. Outbreaks of diseases can occur due to unsanitary conditions and the inability to provide vaccinations and routine healthcare. Additionally, the psychological toll on healthcare workers, who often face threats to their safety and are overwhelmed by the scale of suffering, further diminishes the capacity to respond effectively. The breakdown of health systems illustrates how the ramifications of aggressive military strategies extend far beyond the battlefield.

Ultimately, the humanitarian impacts of conflict underscore the urgent need for a comprehensive approach to peacebuilding that prioritises the welfare of civilians. Aggressive hawkish policies that disregard the human costs of war only serve to fragment world peace further, leading to cycles of violence and instability. Addressing these humanitarian concerns is essential not only for alleviating immediate suffering but also for fostering a sustainable path toward reconciliation and stability. As historical case studies reveal, recognising the human dimension of conflict is crucial in shaping more effective and compassionate diplomatic strategies that can break the cycle of aggression and promote lasting peace.

Economic repercussions on global stability

When a nation adopts a hawkish stance, prioritising military solutions over diplomatic engagement, it often leads to economic instability not only within its borders but also in the international arena. Such aggressive posturing creates an environment of uncertainty and fear, prompting neighbouring countries and global markets to react. Investors may withdraw their capital from regions perceived as volatile, leading to economic downturns. Additionally, countries may impose sanctions on hawkish states, further isolating them economically and creating ripple effects that destabilise global trade networks.

One prominent consequence of aggressive military strategies is the diversion of resources from essential social programs to defence spending. Nations that prioritise military expansion often allocate significant portions of their budgets to armaments and military readiness, leaving less for infrastructure, education, and healthcare. This shift not only undermines the quality of life for citizens but also stifles economic growth. As public discontent rises, internal stability may falter, leading to civil unrest that further strains economic conditions. Such internal turmoil can disrupt not only local markets but also international trade routes, exacerbating global economic instability.

Regional conflicts stemming from hawkish diplomacy often escalate into larger confrontations, further impacting global economic stability. When aggressive nations engage in military confrontations or support insurgent groups, the resulting instability can lead to refugee crises, which strain the economies of neighbouring countries. This influx creates additional burdens on public resources, particularly in healthcare and housing, leading to tensions among host populations. The economic strain can trigger xenophobia and political backlash, resulting in a destabilised region where cooperation is necessary for economic recovery.

Historical case studies illustrate the profound impact of aggressive nations on global economic stability. The Cold War, for instance, showcased how militaristic postures from the United States and the Soviet Union not only shaped their own economies but also influenced global markets. The arms race diverted vast resources, leading to economic challenges that still resonate today. Similarly, more recent conflicts, such as those in the Middle East, demonstrate how military interventions can disrupt oil supplies, leading to significant fluctuations in global oil prices and impacting economies worldwide.

In conclusion, the economic repercussions of hawkish nations on global stability are critical considerations for policymakers and citizens alike. Understanding the interconnectedness of military strategies, regional conflicts, and historical precedents helps illuminate the broader implications of aggressive diplomacy. As nations grapple with the consequences of their actions, it becomes imperative to foster dialogue and cooperation as alternatives to aggression, ensuring a more stable and prosperous global economy.

Environmental consequences of warfare

Warfare has profound and often devastating environmental consequences that extend far beyond the immediate destruction of conflict zones. The physical landscape is altered, ecosystems are disrupted, and biodiversity is severely impacted. Bombing campaigns, for instance, not only obliterate infrastructure but also lead to soil degradation, deforestation, and water contamination. The use of explosives and chemical weapons can render large areas uninhabitable for both humans and wildlife. This destruction contributes to a cycle of environmental degradation that can take decades, if not centuries, to recover from, often leading to further conflict over scarce resources.

In addition to direct destruction, military operations contribute significantly to pollution and climate change. The logistics of warfare involve substantial fuel consumption, which releases greenhouse gases into the atmosphere. Military vehicles, ships, and aircraft are major contributors to carbon emissions, exacerbating global warming. Furthermore, the production and testing of advanced weaponry involve hazardous materials that can contaminate land and water supplies, leading to long-term health issues for local populations. These environmental impacts do not recognise national boundaries, creating regional challenges that can destabilise entire areas and provoke further conflict.

The aftermath of warfare often leaves behind a legacy of environmental issues that disproportionately affect vulnerable communities. In many cases, these communities rely on agriculture, fishing, and natural resources for their livelihoods. The destruction of ecosystems and pollution of water sources can lead to food insecurity and health crises. As these communities struggle to adapt to their degraded environments, tensions can rise, creating fertile ground for new conflicts. The interplay between environmental degradation and social instability illustrates how aggressive military strategies can lead not only to immediate human suffering but also to long-term challenges that threaten regional peace.

Historical case studies provide stark examples of how warfare has led to significant environmental consequences. The Vietnam War, for instance, showcased the devastating effects of herbicides like Agent Orange, which not only destroyed vast areas of forest but also caused lasting damage to human health and biodiversity. Similarly, the Gulf War saw the intentional oil well fires set by retreating forces, which released toxic smoke and pollutants into the atmosphere, contributing to environmental and public health crises that lingered long after the conflict ended. These examples highlight the interconnectedness of warfare and environmental degradation, emphasising the need for a broader understanding of the consequences of aggressive military actions.

Addressing the environmental consequences of warfare requires a multifaceted approach that includes international cooperation and sustainable practices. Nations must recognise that military strategies cannot be divorced from their environmental impacts, and policymakers should incorporate ecological considerations into their defence planning. Efforts to rehabilitate war-torn regions must prioritise environmental restoration as a key component of rebuilding societies. By acknowledging and addressing the environmental consequences of warfare, the international community can take significant steps toward mitigating the fragmentation of world peace caused by aggressive nations.

Chapter 39: Strategies for promoting global peace

Diplomatic solutions and conflict resolution

Diplomatic solutions and conflict resolution play crucial roles in addressing the challenges posed by aggressive nations that disrupt global peace. In a world where military strategies often dominate discussions of international relations, the importance of diplomacy cannot be overstated. Diplomatic efforts aim to create dialogue, foster understanding, and build relationships that can prevent conflicts from escalating. By prioritising negotiation and compromise, nations can work toward sustainable peace, even in the face of hawkish rhetoric and aggressive posturing.

One effective approach to conflict resolution is the use of multilateral diplomacy, where multiple countries come together to address shared concerns. This method allows for diverse perspectives and interests to be considered, promoting a more comprehensive understanding of the issues at hand. Historical case studies, such as the Camp David Accords, illustrate how multilateral negotiations can yield significant progress in resolving tensions. When nations engage in dialogue rather than confrontation, they can often find common ground and develop solutions that benefit all parties involved.

Furthermore, the role of international organisations, such as the United Nations, is pivotal in facilitating diplomatic solutions. These entities provide frameworks for dialogue and conflict resolution, offering platforms for nations to express their grievances and negotiate terms. Peacekeeping missions and mediation efforts by organisations can help de-escalate conflicts and create environments conducive to dialogue. The successful application of these mechanisms can prevent aggressive nations from pursuing military solutions and instead encourage collaborative approaches to conflict.

In addressing regional conflicts stemming from hawkish diplomacy, it is essential to recognise the underlying grievances that fuel tensions. Diplomatic solutions must go beyond mere ceasefires or temporary agreements; they must address the root causes of conflict, including economic disparities, historical grievances, and power imbalances. By engaging in comprehensive peace processes that involve all stakeholders, including marginalised groups, nations can build lasting solutions that reduce the likelihood of future aggression.

Ultimately, the path to peace lies in the commitment of nations to prioritise diplomatic solutions over military aggression. While hawkish strategies may offer short-term gains, they often lead to long-term instability and suffering. By fostering a culture of diplomacy, countries can work together to create a world where dialogue prevails over conflict. This shift in approach is necessary not only for the resolution of current conflicts but also for the prevention of future fragmentation of world peace.

The role of international organisations

International organisations play a crucial role in maintaining global peace and stability, particularly in an era marked by the aggressive posturing of certain nations. These entities, such as the United Nations, NATO, and the African Union, are designed to foster cooperation among countries, promote dialogue, and mediate conflicts. They serve as platforms for diplomacy, providing mechanisms for negotiation and conflict resolution, which are essential in counteracting the fragmentation of world peace caused by hawkish nations. Their ability to bring together diverse stakeholders is vital in managing tensions and addressing the underlying issues that often lead to conflict.

One of the primary functions of international organisations is to establish norms and frameworks that guide state behaviour. Through treaties, conventions, and resolutions, these organisations create a set of expectations for how countries should interact with each other. This normative framework is particularly important when dealing with aggressive nations that may flout international law or engage in militaristic strategies. By holding states accountable to established norms, international organisations can deter aggressive actions and encourage peaceful resolutions to disputes, thereby mitigating the risks of escalation into broader conflicts.

Moreover, international organisations facilitate peacekeeping and conflict resolution efforts in regions experiencing instability due to aggressive diplomacy. Through peacekeeping missions and diplomatic interventions, these organisations can help stabilise volatile situations, protect civilians, and create conditions conducive to dialogue. The effectiveness of such interventions, however, often hinges on the cooperation of the nations involved and their willingness to adhere to international mandates. In cases where hawkish nations resist external intervention, the challenges become significantly more complex, highlighting the limitations of international organisations in enforcing peace.

Historical case studies illustrate the mixed success of international organisations in managing conflicts stemming from aggressive state behaviour. For instance, the United Nations played a pivotal role in mediating the Korean War and later in addressing the tensions on the Korean Peninsula. However, the effectiveness of these interventions has varied, with some conflicts resulting in protracted stalemates despite the presence of international organisations. These case studies underscore the need for a comprehensive understanding of the geopolitical landscape, as well as the motivations of aggressive nations, to enhance the effectiveness of international responses to conflict.

In conclusion, while international organisations are essential in the quest for global peace, their role is often challenged by the actions of hawkish nations. The fragmentation of world peace necessitates a multifaceted approach that includes not only diplomatic engagement but also a commitment to reforming international organisations to better address contemporary conflicts. Strengthening these entities and ensuring their mandates are respected can help create a more stable international order, where aggressive behaviour is curtailed, and dialogue prevails over military strategies. Thus, the collaboration between nations and effective international organisations remains a cornerstone in the ongoing struggle for lasting peace.

Building resilient societies

Building resilient societies in the face of aggressive nations requires a multifaceted approach that recognises the intricate interplay between military strategies, regional conflicts, and the broader global context. Societies that are resilient are not merely those that withstand external pressures; they are also those that adapt, evolve, and foster internal cohesion despite the challenges posed by hawkish diplomacy. The consequences of aggressive actions by nations often manifest in regional instability, leading to a cascade of humanitarian crises, economic decline, and social fragmentation.

One of the primary strategies for building resilience is the promotion of inclusive governance. When societies are governed in a way that includes diverse voices and perspectives, they are better equipped to withstand the divisive tactics often employed by aggressive nations. Inclusive governance fosters trust among citizens and reduces the likelihood of internal conflict, which can be exacerbated by external threats. Furthermore, transparent political processes can help mitigate the influence of hawkish ideologies that seek to manipulate public sentiment for militaristic ends.

Education plays a critical role in fostering resilience as well. By prioritising education that emphasises critical thinking, historical awareness, and global citizenship, societies can cultivate a populace that is less susceptible to fear-based narratives propagated by aggressive nations. An educated citizenry is more inclined to engage in dialogue and seek diplomatic solutions rather than succumbing to militaristic responses. This shift in mindset not only strengthens domestic cohesion but also enhances a society's ability to engage constructively on the international stage.

Economic stability is another pillar of societal resilience. When economies are robust and equitable, communities are less vulnerable to the destabilising effects of external aggression. Economic resilience can be achieved through diversified industries, sustainable practices, and equitable distribution of resources. By investing in local economies and fostering regional cooperation, societies can create a buffer against the economic disruptions often instigated by hawkish nations. This stability not only supports internal cohesion but also diminishes the leverage that aggressive nations may have over vulnerable economies.

Finally, fostering strong civil society organisations is essential for building resilience. These organisations play a crucial role in promoting social cohesion, advocating for human rights, and providing support during crises. They can serve as a counterbalance to hawkish narratives by promoting peacebuilding initiatives and community engagement. By empowering civil society, nations can cultivate a culture of resilience that actively challenges the fragmentation caused by aggressive diplomacy. Through collaboration, dialogue, and a commitment to shared values, societies can emerge stronger and more united in the face of external threats, ultimately contributing to a more peaceful global landscape.

Chapter 40: Conclusion: Navigating the future

Lessons learned from historical patterns
Historical patterns provide critical insights into the behaviour of aggressive nations and their impact on global peace. By examining past conflicts and diplomatic strategies, we can identify recurring themes that illustrate how hawkish nations often pursue aggressive policies, leading to fragmentation in international relations. These lessons underscore the importance of understanding historical context when analysing current geopolitical tensions and the potential for future conflicts.

One notable pattern is the tendency of aggressive nations to leverage military strategies as a primary means of achieving their objectives. Historical case studies, such as the expansionist policies of Nazi Germany or the imperial ambitions of Japan prior to World War II, demonstrate that military might is frequently prioritised over diplomatic engagement. These nations often viewed conflict as a viable tool for resolving disputes or expanding influence, disregarding the long-term consequences of their actions. The repercussions of such strategies often resulted in widespread devastation and a significant deterioration in global peace.

Case studies of aggressive nations reveal additional lessons about the fragility of peace in the face of militaristic diplomacy. The Balkan Wars of the 1990s highlight how ethnic tensions and nationalistic fervour, often fuelled by hawkish rhetoric, can lead to brutal conflicts and humanitarian crises. The dissolution of Yugoslavia demonstrates that when aggressive nations prioritise territorial claims over cooperative solutions, the consequences can be catastrophic, leading to protracted violence and deep-seated animosities that persist for generations.

In conclusion, the lessons learned from historical patterns of aggressive nations illustrate the profound impact of militaristic strategies on global peace. Understanding these patterns is essential for policymakers and the public alike, as they offer valuable insights into the motivations and consequences of hawkish diplomacy. By reflecting on the past, we can better navigate the complexities of modern international relations and strive towards a more peaceful and cooperative global community.

The path forward for global cooperation

The path forward for global cooperation requires a multifaceted approach that acknowledges the complexities of international relations shaped by aggressive nations. These hawkish states often prioritise military strength and aggressive diplomacy, leading to fragmentation and instability in world peace. To counteract these trends, it is essential to foster dialogue and collaboration among nations, focusing on shared interests and common goals. Emphasising mutual respect and understanding can help build bridges that transcend the divides created by aggressive posturing.

One of the critical steps in promoting global cooperation is the establishment of robust diplomatic channels. Countries must prioritise open communication to address grievances and misunderstandings that often fuel conflicts. Regular dialogues, peace summits, and international forums can serve as platforms for negotiation and conflict resolution. Engaging in confidence-building measures can enhance trust among nations, reducing the likelihood of miscalculations that could lead to military confrontations. By investing in diplomacy, nations can work together to create a more stable and peaceful global environment.

Economic cooperation is another vital component in the path forward for global collaboration. By promoting trade agreements and economic partnerships, nations can create interdependencies that make conflict less desirable. Economic ties can serve as a deterrent against aggression, as nations recognise the mutual benefits of maintaining peaceful relations. Additionally, investment in joint initiatives—such as infrastructure development, climate change mitigation, and humanitarian efforts—can strengthen relationships, demonstrating that collaboration yields tangible benefits for all parties involved.

Finally, Institutions such as the United Nations, NATO, and regional bodies provide frameworks for collective action and conflict resolution. These organisations must adapt to the evolving geopolitical landscape by enhancing their capacity to respond to aggression and fostering a culture of accountability. Strengthening global governance structures can ensure that aggressive nations face consequences for their actions while simultaneously providing avenues for peaceful dispute resolution. Through a concerted effort to reinforce these mechanisms, the international community can work towards a more cooperative and peaceful world.

Final thoughts on the role of the public in peacebuilding

Final thoughts on the role of the public in peacebuilding highlight the critical importance of civic engagement in addressing the challenges posed by aggressive nations. The public's awareness and understanding of the implications of hawkish policies are essential for fostering a culture of peace. When citizens are informed about the effects of aggressive military strategies and the resulting fragmentation of world peace, they are better equipped to advocate for diplomatic solutions and peaceful coexistence. Public sentiment can influence policymakers, compelling them to consider alternatives to military engagement and to prioritise dialogue over conflict.

The role of grassroots movements in peacebuilding is paramount. History has shown that organised civilian efforts can effectively challenge the narratives propagated by aggressive nations. These movements often serve as a powerful counterbalance to hawkish diplomacy, emphasising the need for cooperative approaches to regional conflicts. By raising awareness about the consequences of militarisation and promoting peace initiatives, the public can create a groundswell of support for policies that prioritise negotiation and reconciliation. This active participation is crucial for shifting the focus from military solutions to sustainable peacebuilding practices.

Civic engagement extends beyond grassroots movements and education; it also includes the use of technology and social media to amplify voices advocating for peace. In today's interconnected world, the public can leverage digital platforms to share information, mobilise support, and hold governments accountable for their actions. This capability enables a global dialogue about the repercussions of militaristic strategies and the necessity of pursuing peaceful resolutions to conflicts. By utilising these tools effectively, citizens can contribute to a more informed and active public discourse surrounding peacebuilding.

Ultimately, the public's role in peacebuilding is foundational to counteracting the fragmentation caused by aggressive nations. As citizens become more engaged and informed, they can challenge hawkish narratives and advocate for policies that promote stability and harmony. The potential for transformative change lies within the collective actions of the public, demonstrating that peacebuilding is not solely the responsibility of governments but a shared obligation that requires the participation and commitment of every individual. By embracing this responsibility, the public can play a decisive role in shaping a more peaceful future.

References:

Necessary readings

1) Treaty of Westphalia in 1648 established key principles of state sovereignty and non-interference, which still serve as foundational elements in international relations today.

2) In Somalia, the U.S.-led intervention in the early 1990s aimed to alleviate famine and restore order but resulted in a protracted civil war and a humanitarian crisis that continues to this day. In Iraq, weapons of mass destruction, Afghanistan, Granada, Libya, Vietnam, Korea etc.

3} The military actions in Libya in 2011, aimed at overthrowing a dictatorial regime, resulted in chaos and ongoing conflict, raising questions about the responsibility of superpowers in creating a sustainable peace.

4) The Marshall Plan, which aimed to rebuild war-torn European economies, illustrates how peace can catalyse economic recovery and cooperation.

5) Good Friday Agreement in Northern Ireland, demonstrate that establishing trust between conflicting parties is essential for moving forward.

6) The legal framework governing occupation is primarily derived from the Hague Conventions of 1899 and 1907, along with the Fourth Geneva Convention of 1949.

7) The principles governing occupation are primarily derived from the Hague Conventions of 1899 and 1907, which established rules for the conduct of war and the treatment of occupied territories.

8) The United Nation Charter's Article 2(4) explicitly prohibits the threat or use of force against the territorial integrity or political independence of any state

9) Vietnam in the 1960s

10) The Soviet Union's intervention in Afghanistan from 1979 to 1989

11) NATO's involvement in the Balkans during the 1990s

12) in 2003, led by the United States, was justified on the grounds of dismantling weapons of mass destruction

13) In Libya, the 2011 intervention

14) Military interventions in various contexts, with Syria

15) The establishment of the State of Israel in 1948

16) The legal framework governing occupation is primarily derived from the Hague Conventions of 1899 and 1907, along with the Fourth Geneva Convention of 1949

17) Warsaw Pact in 1955 further institutionalised this bloc, fostering military cooperation among the Eastern European states and presenting a unified front against NATO

Also by DM Ole Kiminta

How the Western Democracies failed the world
Supporting Refugees in their Homelands
Dissuading Global War Mongers:
Dissuading war mongers
La Libération Monétaire en Afrique
Canada Post: Management failure to modernise mail systems
Canada Post management failure to modernise mail systems
Canada Post: Management failure to modernise mail systems
Live to be 200
Aim to live for 200
Aim to live to be 200
Western democracies failed the world economies
Wrong foot forward: US-Canada trade wars
Canada begs to differ: Never a 51st state of USA
Tethered to the Kitchen
Nous ne pouvons pas être le 51e État des États-Unis
Nous ne serons jamais le 51ème état des États-Unis.
The Nephilim and the erosion of moral boundaries
Every human is an advocate for World Peace
The diplomatic dilemma of Western Sahara
Every human: Advocate for World Peace

About the Author

DM Ole Kiminta is a Canadian of Maasai heritage. He spent many years working in USA, Britain and in Canada. He is an Industrial engineer, Petroleum engineer and Chemical engineer. Ole Kiminta was educated in USA and United Kingdom. Some of his published research work include Material science, carbon fibres and other composite materials, Polymeric materials, and Particle technology. He currently works for the Canadian government and lives in Toronto Canada with his family.

www.ingramcontent.com/pod-product-compliance
Lightning Source LLC
Chambersburg PA
CBHW022336280326
41934CB00006B/655